ULTIM
SPORTS

DINA ASHER-SMITH

KATARINA JOHNSON- THOMPSON

GOING FOR GOLD

DINO

First published by Dino Books in 2021
an imprint of Bonnier Books UK,
4th Floor, Victoria House, Bloomsbury Square, London WC1B 4DA
Owned by Bonnier Books,
Sveavägen 56, Stockholm, Sweden

 @dinobooks
www.bonnierbooks.co.uk

© Dino Books
Dina Asher-Smith written by Charlotte Browne
Katarina Johnson-Thompson written by Melanie Hamm
Cover illustration by Bruce Huang

Paperback ISBN: 9781789465655

British Library cataloguing-in-publication data:
A catalogue record for this book is available from the British Library.

Printed and bound in Great Britain by Clays Ltd, Elcograf S.p.A.

1 3 5 7 9 10 8 6 4 2

MIX
Paper from
responsible sources
FSC® C018072

DINA ASHER-SMITH

TABLE OF CONTENTS

CHAPTER 1

STRAIGHT INTO THE DUCK POND

Winston Asher-Smith breathed a deep sigh of satisfaction as he walked through the chalk meadows and woodlands of High Elms Country Park in Orpington. He stopped and turned to his wife, Julie, and the two of them took in the beautiful view towards the North Downs that stretched before them.

'It's such a relief we have this on our doorstep. It makes the commute into London each day just about bearable, knowing we can come here at the weekends.'

Winston worked as a mechanical engineer in the

city, and like most other commuters, he struggled with the daily grind.

'When you're squeezed into a tube train with someone's armpit in your face, I try and imagine I'm walking through the fields here.'

Julie looked at him and laughed. 'That can't be easy to imagine!' She looked off into the distance thoughtfully. 'Sometimes when the wind rushes through the branches here, I pretend it's the sound of the sea. And just for a second I fool myself that I can smell the coffee growing, wafting down from the Blue Mountains.'

He looked at her and smiled. 'Yes, the sea, I miss it too.'

Winston and Julie were both originally from Jamaica but had made the UK their home.

'There is Kingston in Shoreham of course, down on the south coast. That's only 20 minutes away,' said Julie.

They both laughed.

'Not sure I'd get in the sea there any time of year

– even during a heatwave! Brrr!' said Winston.

'Yeah, we don't have many of those here, but at least we don't have to worry about hurricane season.'

'Good point,' Winston sighed. 'But I do miss my sprint days, running along the beach.'

'Mama!'

They stopped to both look down at their two-year-old daughter, Dina, who was starting to get agitated and restless in her pushchair. She was looking up at them impatiently, her big brown eyes imploring them to take her out.

'What is it, apple pie?' her father asked. Dina's grandmother had coined this nickname because she thought her grandchild had the sweetest smile she'd ever seen, with the sweetest nature to match. The name had stuck. But, from the moment Dina had learnt to crawl, she had been an active child and her sunny nature could change if she was put in a pushchair or buggy for too long.

'We'd better take her out now,' said Julie. 'She

won't sleep otherwise.'

She bent down to undo the straps on Dina's chair and said: 'You don't like being cooped up for too long, do you?'

Dina beamed as she began to wriggle free, and Julie added: 'You never seem to get tired on those legs of yours either!'

'Hardly a surprise is it? What with my athletic prowess,' Winston chuckled.

'Er, excuse me, I was a demon on that hockey pitch back in the day. I used to run rings round the other team. In fact, when Dina's a little older, I'll start teaching her.'

'Yeah, but it's not real running, is it, just a bit of skipping about.'

'What?! I'm an excellent runner! I did a great time in the 800-metre race with the Herne Hill Harriers.'

'Amateurs!'

'At least I still run. You're so out of practice I bet I'd hardly have to lift a finger against you in a sprint now.'

'We'll see about that. Race you to that tree!' Winston pointed in the direction of a giant oak just over a hundred metres away.

'Easy!' Julie laughed and went to bend down as if at a starting block. She then turned round in a panic.

'Dina? Dina?!'

While they teased each other, Dina had taken the chance to climb out of her buggy and make a bolt for freedom.

'There she is!'

Winston pointed towards Dina, who was heading off in the distance towards a duck pond at the foot of the hills. She was toddling at great speed and had already covered a lot of ground. They both sped after her, no longer concerned with who got there first.

Dina stopped for a second and looked back at them, laughing, her eyes shining.

'Quack, quack!' She pointed at the ducks, her

short, dark curls bouncing, and sped on towards the edge of the pond.

Her parents shouted after her. A couple of onlookers watched in shock as she accelerated. One rushed forward in an attempt to reach her but couldn't catch her before her legs reached the water. She showed no sign of slowing down as she went splashing into the shallow depths of the pond, still laughing at the startled ducks, who noisily flew away in a cloud of feathers.

Winston waded into the pond and lifted Dina out. He reassured Julie, who was just behind him: 'Don't worry, it's not too deep.'

'Dina, are you alright?! Who knows what's in that pond!'

'She seems okay, just rather wet!'

As Dina took in the angry and serious faces of her breathless parents, her joyful expression crumpled.

'Oh Dina – it's alright!' They both comforted her as she burst into tears. 'But don't ever do that again!'

She turned back to look at the ducks. 'Splash, splash!'

'I've never seen a little kid run so fast!' They both turned around to see the shocked face of one of the passers-by.

'Neither have we!' said Dina's parents in unison.

'You've got your work cut out for you, running around after that one.'

'She couldn't wait to get in the water!'

Julie and Winston turned to face each other.

'I think we might have to think about swimming lessons.'

'Or sort out some sort of alarm system if she runs over a metre! We can't let her out of our sight for a second!'

CHAPTER 2

SPORTS DAY

Dina took a deep breath and began to blow into her trumpet, determined to nail the tricky intro to the *William Tell* Overture. She sighed in frustration as she fumbled over the first few notes for the third time. Her teacher looked at her in surprise.

'Everything alright, Dina?'

'Yep. Sorry, I'll try again.' Dina always stuck at things if she didn't get them right the first time. From firing golf balls into the flowerpots at the back of the garden with her dad to scoring against her mum when they played hockey together on the street, she always told herself: 'I'll try harder next time, until I get it right.'

She normally loved playing the trumpet, but she couldn't focus that morning. She kept gazing out of the window of her school's music block. It was a beautiful sunny day with a gentle breeze blowing. Just perfect for Perry Hall Primary School's sports day. She was almost too excited at the prospect of running that afternoon for her sports team in the relay race. It was her first year at primary school and Miss Papadopoulos had asked her to run the last leg, or anchor, of the race for their house team, which was a mix of students from different year groups in the school: 'You're the anchor, Dina!'

Dina knew her teacher had noticed how fast she ran and that she'd been chosen to make the difference on those vital last metres of the home stretch. She also knew her mum would be watching that afternoon and she wanted to make her proud too. She felt a mixture of fear and excitement and vowed to run the best that she could for the team. 'I want us to win,' she said to herself over and over.

'I want to win.'

She barely managed to contain her excitement for the rest of the lesson. She normally wolfed down her chicken drumsticks at lunch, but on this occasion she could only pick at them. As she was changing into her PE kit, her friends chattered and laughed around her in the school's changing rooms, while she felt her nerves rising. Wow, why weren't they more nervous? They didn't seem that bothered about winning.

Her friend Nicole put her arm around her. 'Dina, don't worry, you'll smash it for us.'

Dina smiled back and laughed but could feel the adrenaline rising inside her.

'It's just a race,' Nicole added.

Dina laughed and shrugged. 'Sure, I know.'

But deep down she knew it meant something to her. It always meant something to her. Whether she was swimming, playing hockey, dancing or playing the trumpet, she wanted to win and enjoyed it when she did. She walked out to the field thinking of her idol, Serena Williams, and tried to imagine how she must feel walking out on to the court each time. Her heart beat a little faster as she remembered something that she'd heard Serena say in an interview. 'Tennis is mostly mental. You win or lose the match before you even go out there.' Dina imagined how good she would feel crossing the line first and smiled to herself. She instantly felt a little calmer.

Dina cheered on her teammates who blitzed their way through the egg-and-spoon race, bean bag throwing competition and the hula hoop challenge. Miss Papadopoulos jumped up and down with excitement too as they picked up top points throughout. But then they faced tough competition from some seasoned sprinters in the upper school and fell behind by several points. It was time for the 4 x 100 metres relay race, the last race. Miss Papadopoulos gathered Dina and her three other teammates together.

'Okay guys, who wants to win the cup for

our house?!'

'Me!' They all shouted in unison.

'Okay! So just remember: don't look behind for the baton, just wait until you feel it in your hands, look straight ahead and run! You can do this!'

Dina took her place on the track. She knew how tricky baton changes were from watching them on the TV; it was a hard technique to perfect in athletics because of the speed of the runners. The crowd cheered as the first leg took off and Dina beamed as she heard her mum rooting for each runner on her team.

The first runner hadn't made a great start and was trailing behind in fourth place by the time the second runner took the baton. Dina watched the second runner's ponytail swish from side to side as she made up some ground to take third before passing to the third runner.

While Dina cheered, she thought to herself, *not long now*. She had her work cut out for her, as two of the runners had already changed over, but she knew she was a fast sprinter and that she could make a difference in this last leg.

She waited with bated breath while the runner on the third leg ran down the field towards her, the baton glinting in the afternoon sun. She held out her left palm as straight as possible for the handover. The second she felt the baton in her hand she gripped it as tightly as possible before sprinting down the field.

'Go Dina!' she heard her team cheer. She made up a lot of ground on the two who'd taken the lead, their T-shirts flailing behind them in the wind.

'I can catch them,' she said to herself. At 10 metres, then 20 metres, she was hot on their heels. She felt amazing, as though her body was gliding through the air. She broke out into a smile as she overtook each runner, one by one, until she effortlessly crossed the finish line. She threw her hands behind, like the serious athletes she'd seen on the TV. Then she caught sight of her mum jumping up and down for joy among the crowd of mums that had gathered at the front, their jaws agape in astonishment. Then she heard Miss Papadopoulos's voice: 'Dina, that was incredible! You flew like the wind!'

She felt her teammates' arms around her, lifting her up and cheering: 'Dina! Dina!' They'd done it. She'd done it. As her team lifted the winning trophy, she knew she'd been important in their win. And this was a feeling she wanted more of.

CHAPTER 3

RUNNING CLUB

'Race you to the swings!'

'What's the point Dina, you're too fast!'

But it was too late. Dina had already shot off ahead of her friend Nicole down the path through Poverest Park, her two plaits flying behind her in the wind. Located just behind Dina's house and next to her school, it provided a wide-open space for them to play in.

Nicole caught up with Dina, who was already sitting on the swing, her brown eyes twinkling as she leisurely swung her feet, smiling joyfully. Nicole knew there was no smugness or spite in her expression; Dina just loved running, simple as that.

'You're not even out of breath!' gasped Nicole.

'It's all the swimming I do. My teacher says it keeps my lungs strong.'

Dina was never one to brag about her talent, and Nicole smiled. She had a suggestion to make: 'You should join the school's running club.'

Dina shrugged. 'I dunno.'

It was a few days after sports day and her friends were still talking about Dina's run. But she wasn't sure if she wanted to join another club. From dancing to diving and Brownies, she loved to take part in many different sports and activities.

'Come with me this Monday lunchtime,' said Nicole.

'Maybe.'

'Oh, go on! I'll buy you an ice cream if you do!'

A smile spread over Dina's face. Nicole knew how to persuade her. Frozen treats of any flavour were a staple favourite.

'What, now?'

Nicole sighed and felt around for loose change in her pocket. 'If it gets you to running club.'

'Race you to the ice cream van then!'

* * *

Dina spent the morning gazing out of the window at the school's field track. Her class were learning about the Ancient Greeks. She found this period of history fascinating; in particular she loved to read the myths and learn about the strength and power that the gods and goddesses possessed. When she got home from school she excitedly recounted some of her favourite stories to her parents: Theseus slaying the Minotaur, Icarus flying too close to the sun or Athena beating Poseidon to become the patron goddess of Athens.

She sighed and thought to herself: 'I reckon it would be alright to be a god or goddess. They definitely had lots of fun and could do all sorts of things with their strength and power.' She thought about the modern-day heroes she admired: Serena Williams, Kelly Holmes. They might not be able to make fire, whip up storms or fight monsters, but they were the closest equivalent that she could think of.

Learning about the Ancient Greeks wasn't the only reason she loved Mondays though. As the clock ticked towards lunchtime, she grew more and more excited. She couldn't wait to get out on to the track for running club.

In her first week at the club her teacher, Mrs Carty, was taken aback by Dina's speed. After a quick warm-up, she gave some pointers on the best way to run: 'Keep your upper body as relaxed as possible and don't expel all your energy to begin with.'

Then, Mrs Carty encouraged the children to run along beside her as they took on the first lap of the field.

'Okay, now go at your own pace, gently does it to start. Don't put pressure on yourself to keep up with me.'

She started off at a steady pace with 10 girls following behind her before she increased her speed. Before long, she heard the sound of someone's feet pounding behind her. She turned to look just as Dina drew up beside her, a broad smile slowly spreading across her face.

'Hi, Miss!' she said.

'Hi Dina! Are you enjoying your first day at running club?' She asked the question with a knowing smile. The answer was already clear.

As the weeks progressed, Dina started to overtake her teacher with seemingly little effort, and Mrs Carty found herself struggling to keep up with her.

'Hi again, Miss!' she quipped as she ran past her for the second and third time round the lap.

On one occasion, she admitted to Dina: 'I never thought I'd struggle to keep up with a seven-year-old child but you really are fast!' Although she was cautious not to praise Dina too much, she also noticed the girl's humility; during running club,

Dina was kind to the other children and gave them advice on how to warm up their muscles.

The teachers could see that Dina was in her element when she ran around the field and loved the opportunity to shine. Dina was enjoying running more and more, although she still enjoyed all her other hobbies. However, that summer her parents encouraged her to try out other track and field events. On the first day of the holidays, Dina headed for Perry Hall's athletics club. Her eyes lit up as she saw the size of the field track with its proper white lane markings, just like the ones she saw in the stadiums on TV, as well as the sand-filled runway and horizontal bar for long jump and high jump. In the distance, she saw children practising their javelin and discus throws.

One afternoon their teacher, Mr Hewitt, set out six hurdles for the children to practise as a warm-up. Dina smiled as she saw the obstacles stretching out before her. She couldn't wait to leap over them.

Mr Hewitt instructed them: 'Stay tall, keep your

body forward and don't lean back. Bend and lift with your knee.' Dina could barely take his words in as she sized up the height of them and got in her lane alongside the other children.

'On your marks, get set – go!'

Dina tore off down the track towards the first hurdle, and bounced over it lightly, lifting her right knee instinctively. She cleared the next three gleefully before running towards the finishing line. She looked back to see the other children behind her, either knocking the hurdles over or plodding cautiously over each one. Mr Hewitt shook his head in amazement.

At the end of the day, Dina bounded over to her mother with a huge smile on her face. 'That was so much fun!'

'What did you enjoy the most?'

'All of it! But I really loved the hurdles.'

Mr Hewitt walked over to speak to them both.

'She flew over them like a gazelle!' he said, shaking his head in disbelief. 'You don't have springs in your feet do you, Dina?'

Dina's mother laughed.

'No, they're just ordinary trainers, I promise,' said Dina.

'Well, if you approach all your events as you approached those hurdles, you've got a bright future ahead of you as an athlete.'

Dina smiled at these words. She thought of all the athletes she watched on TV. For now, running was just for fun. But could she be just like one of them, one day? Her heart soared at the thought of it.

CHAPTER 4

THE
BEES

It was a cold and wet November morning and there was a mist descending around the lake in Crystal Palace Park. As Dina trampled through the mud and soggy wet leaves on the ground, she began to regret agreeing to take part in the Bromley Primary Schools Cross Country Championships. This was the third time her PE teacher, Miss Hudson, had picked her, and she knew it was because she was good. Up against 54 other primary schools, Dina helped her school team finish near the top five and had consistently finished in some of the highest places across the county.

She shivered as she felt the damp seep through her waterproof running jacket and thought gratefully of the hot chocolate and treats she knew would be awaiting her at the finishing line. Crowds had lined the route to cheer on the runners. Dina vowed this would be the last time she ran long distance. No amount of coaxing from Miss Hudson would persuade her again.

She groaned to herself as she continued to trudge through the mud. 'When will this end?'

But it wasn't long before the cheers from the crowd grew even louder and she realised she was approaching the last hundred metres. 'Not long till my hot chocolate!' This comforting thought spurred her on past the finishing line. As she crossed it, she saw Mrs Carty and Miss Hudson cheering and waving at her, huddled together under an umbrella. Then she saw her mum, who looked even more excited than usual. Her dad was just behind her, chatting away to people in the crowds but, as always, keeping a look out for Dina.

Her mum rushed forward to hug her, swiftly followed by her dad. 'You've won!'

'What?' Dina was gobsmacked.

Her mum handed her a cup of hot chocolate and threw a big fleece-lined sou'wester around her. 'Well done, Dina! I think you've finished even faster than last time – just under 20 minutes!'

Miss Hudson and Mrs Carty came over to congratulate her too.

'One of the fastest times in the whole county, I bet!' said Miss Hudson.

Dina was very happy to win, but then she remembered the promise she'd made to herself. She stared at the four of them defiantly, as the rain continued to beat down.

'I've had enough of this. I'm not doing it again.'

'Ah Dina, once you've warmed up you'll change your mind,' said Miss Hudson.

'No, I love running. But I don't want to do long distance. I just want to sprint from now on.'

She'd never said it out loud before but suddenly

it completely made sense to her.

The four of them looked at her and then nodded their heads in agreement.

'When you sprint, you always have a smile on your face,' said her mother. 'I'd rather you did that if it makes you happy.'

'Yeah,' said her dad, 'you do look a bit grumpy at the moment!'

'You would if you'd just been running through 1800 metres of mud and sludge!' said her mum.

'Congratulations, Dina!'

Dina heard a friendly voice behind her. She turned around and looked up to see an equally friendly face of a man she'd never seen before.

'Not a nice day to be running, eh. Have you warmed up yet?'

Dina's hands were gripping her hot chocolate. 'Just about.' She smiled.

He held his hand out to Dina's parents. 'Hi, I'm John. I'm from Blackheath and Bromley Harriers. Have you heard of us?'

They all nodded. Dina most certainly had. The athletics club was one of the oldest in south-east London and was known for producing a fair number of sporting legends.

'Well, I just wanted to congratulate your daughter on an incredible run.'

'Thank you.'

He turned back to Dina. 'How would you feel about joining our athletics club?'

'Blackheath and Bromley?'

'You're a bit too young for the big club just now, I'm afraid. But we could start you at the Bromley Bees.'

Dina looked at her parents.

'Mum? Dad?'

They both smiled at her. 'Well, it's your decision. Would you like to join?'

Dina nodded her head enthusiastically.

'Yes! I'd love to!'

Then a look of doubt crossed her face and she turned back to John. 'You won't make me do cross country, will you?!'

'You don't want to do it? Even though you're so good at it?'

'No! Never again.'

John laughed. 'Well I haven't seen you on field and track yet.'

He crossed his arms and looked at her with a twinkle in his eye. 'How do I know you're any good?'

Mrs Carty piped up, 'Oh, she is, I can tell you! Flies faster than the wind!'

'Well,' replied John, 'I look forward to working with you at The Bees.'

CHAPTER 5

OLYMPIC DREAMS

Dina felt her skin tingle. She watched Kelly Holmes prepare to settle into the starting block. She had a look of cool, calm concentration on her face as she stared down the track.

It was the 2004 Athens Olympics and Dina was so nervous that even her favourite hot chicken wings sat uneaten by her side. Kelly had been troubled by leg injuries in the year running up to the Olympics, but she was still favourite for the gold medal in the 800 metres. However, it would be a tight race against three-time world champion Maria de Lurdes Mutola. Kelly had never been able to beat her.

Eight-year-old Dina couldn't imagine what was going through Kelly's head as the gun fired for the start of the race. Kelly had come out of retirement and, at the age of 34, was giving the Olympics one last shot. The commentators and the whole of Britain were behind her. Just two minutes of running lay ahead of her but everyone knew how much winning a medal would mean to her.

Dina and her parents sat glued to the television as Kelly approached the final lap. She was still in last place, steadily striding behind eight other runners.

'She's trailing at the back at the moment but I don't think she will for much longer!' said the commentator, and Dina clung to their hopeful words.

'I can't watch!' Dina's mum fled the room.

'Oh, Julie, you can't miss her becoming an Olympic champion!' Dina's dad was optimistic.

'Just call me back in if she's doing well!'

'She's pacing, Mum, she's pacing!' Dina called after her. She knew how important this was in any long-distance race. She took her eyes off the screen for a second before turning back to watch Kelly, who began attacking on the outside, and gaining ground on her nemesis, Maria.

'She's in it, Julie – she's back in it!'

'What?!' Julie hurried back to the doorway of the lounge.

'Oh wow – would you look at that!' Kelly had levelled with world champions Hasna Benhassi and Jolanda Čeplak. They were just 50 metres from the finish and approaching the final bend.

'Come on Kelly – come on!' The three of them were up on their feet cheering her on with the crowd as she sped down the final lap to challenge Maria in the lead.

'It's so close!' cried Julie.

'She's gonna do it!' said Winston.

'Come on, Kelly!' Dina roared at the TV. She held her breath as she watched her battle to overtake Maria, Hasna still threatening from the outside. Then she leapt for joy as Kelly scraped the finishing line to take first place, with Hasna in second and Jolanda flying from behind to finish third.

'She's done it!'

'Just wonderful!'

'What a performance!'

The three of them jumped around and hugged each other.

It was one of the tightest 800-metre races for women in Olympic history. They saw a look of confusion pass over Kelly's face, because she was still unsure if she was first across the line. Tears filled Dina's eyes as the commentator screamed their congratulations at the top of their lungs, and she saw the pure elation on Kelly's face as she realised she'd taken gold for Britain.

Kelly had won by five hundredths of a second in a new world record time of 1 minute 56 seconds. Her long wait to be an Olympic champion was over and Dina had a new hero.

Five nights later Dina watched her fall to the ground in disbelief after she won the 1500 metres final with a personal best of 3 minutes 57 seconds. It was her second Olympic gold medal, achieved against the odds.

'Just incredible,' said Julie. 'The oldest woman to ever win either race, let alone both!'

'And the first British athlete to win a double Olympic gold in both races for 80 years!' said Winston.

Dina watched Kelly struggle to hold back her emotions as she stood on the podium wrapped in the British flag, her gold medal around her neck. When the British national anthem ended, she waved to the crowd. Dina was particularly captivated by the laurel wreath that Kelly was wearing. She looked just like the Greek goddesses she learnt about at school.

'You know, Mum, the wreath is a symbol of triumph! Apollo wore one! And it's what they always used to give to the athletes when they won!'

Julie replied: 'Looks as though it gets in the way a bit, though!' They both laughed as Kelly's wreath slipped down her forehead, momentarily distracting her.

Dina imagined how it would feel to stand on the highest platform of the podium, winning gold for Great Britain and waving to the crowds. And how cool it would be to wear a wreath! If this was the closest she could get to being a Greek goddess, she'd give it a shot! Whatever it took!

That night she took out some coloured crayons and drew a picture of herself upon an Olympic tri-level podium. It was an ordinary enough looking picture of her in sportswear, but there were two finishing touches. Firstly, she added a laurel wreath. She held it up, admiring her handiwork. Finally, she took a pen and wrote in capitals underneath: I WANT TO BE AN OLYMPIC CHAMPION.

CHAPTER 6

HOLDING THE HORSES

'It's Saturday!' Every weekend Dina leapt out of bed and threw on her black and orange Bromley Bees Academy kit and matching trainers. She was filled with excitement at the thought of another fun day at Norman Park Athletics Track.

As club founder, Mick Jones, explained to the children who attended the club, they were there to learn the basics of running, jumping and throwing to give them a broad exposure to athletics. One of Dina's favourite events was the long jump. As she pelted down the runway towards the sandpit, she loved the feeling of acceleration in her feet before she propelled herself forward.

'Wheeee!' she shouted, flying through the air with a huge smile on her face before she landed in the sand. It was the closest she came to feeling like she was flying. She was also good at it. As the weeks went by, her jumping distance grew from four to six feet, improving her personal best each time. Dina had also made friends with a girl called Shannon Hylton, who loved sprinting just as much as she did.

One Saturday, after she'd jumped nearly 10 feet, John drew her aside.

'Well, your teacher was right – you can definitely run!'

Dina beamed.

'But more specifically than that, I think you're a sprinter.' John was particularly impressed with the ground she could cover in a short space of time on the long-jump runway. Dina's heart soared at these words, just as it did when she flew down the track with the wind in her hair.

'How about we try you out in some 100- and 200-metre races with the other kids?'

Dina nodded enthusiastically.

Mick and John watched in amazement as she tore round the track, overtaking all the other children. Some were older than her and had been training at the club for several years.

Mick said: 'She's just so...'

'"Springy" is the only word I can think of,' said John.

'If she keeps progressing like this, she'll be through to the Blackheath and Bromley club in no time,' said John.

Mick turned to him. 'What do you think about coaching her, John? Think she's got the potential to go far?'

John paused for a moment. 'I think she's got it in her to go all the way,' he replied.

Mick looked surprised. 'I don't think I've seen you this sure about anyone for a long time.'

'Well, we'll have to see, of course. But my

instinct is that she's got the attitude to match her talent.'

'Olympic champion?'

'Quite possibly.'

Mick whistled. 'Well, if that's what you think, then we need to invest in her.'

After Dina crossed the finishing line, John beckoned her over. 'We're very impressed with how you've developed here. As well as your natural sprinting ability, you've got good agility, balance and coordination too.'

Dina smiled. 'Thank you,' she said.

'But,' John said quickly, 'do you want to become even faster?'

Dina nodded her head vigorously.

He continued. 'It's all good being naturally gifted, but about 70 per cent of speed is down to training and technique.'

'If you'd like to, I think we can take your training up to the next level. How would you feel about putting in some extra hours of coaching each week?

Here at the track, with me?'

Dina's eyes lit up. 'Yes please!'

'If your parents agree, we'll put together a plan to start working towards some national competitions.'

Dina's eyes widened. 'Really?'

'Yes, I think you're ready. Although I'll never push you to do anything I don't think you're ready for.'

'Are you going to get me pumping iron in the gym then?'

'Hmm, no, I'll go easy on you for now, you're still growing. Just some simple strength training using resistance bands.'

'That's what Apollo must have done, I reckon.'

'Ha! Well yes, the gods were pretty blessed in that way. They didn't have to work for their superhero powers, they just had them. But us mere mortals have to work for it!'

She thought of Kelly Holmes standing up on the podium and the picture she'd drawn. Was she prepared to work for it? She still enjoyed swimming and playing hockey every week. Would this take time away from that? Plus, it wasn't long until she started big school.

John read her mind. 'Now, I know your mum is a little concerned this might impact your homework when you start secondary school. What are your thoughts?'

Dina thought about it. She loved athletics but she also loved learning. She would find a way.

She nodded determinedly and said: 'I can do both.'

John smiled. 'That's what I thought. You're not one to hold the horses.'

'Hold the what?'

He laughed. 'Don't hold the horses. It's one of my favourite phrases. You'll find out soon enough.'

CHAPTER 7

DARREN CAMPBELL

Dina gazed out towards the field she'd run around on sports day and down the road towards Poverest Park. It was her last day at Perry Hall Primary before she moved to secondary school and she wanted to soak up the childhood memories.

'Dina!' Nicole's voice brought her back to earth. 'You haven't signed my jumper yet!' Nicole headed towards her, her school jumper covered in scrawls and signatures. 'I definitely want yours! It'll be worth a fortune one day when you're an Olympic champion!'

Dina laughed. 'Well, if that does happen, I'll

have you to thank, I suppose!' She thought back to the day in Poverest Park when Nicole bought her an ice cream.

'Oh, whatever!' said Nicole. Dina's humility always amazed her.

Miss Hudson and Mrs Carty gave Dina a big goodbye hug. She struggled to hold back the tears. There were so many happy memories from her school and these teachers, the first to encourage her running, were still so supportive:

'You're going to love it there. You'll be doing big proper history lessons now, where you'll get to learn about more than just the Ancient Greeks. You'll be a fountain of knowledge before long.'

'Yes, you'll know more than us in no time!'

'Now, we don't want you to come back and see us till you're a big running star, okay?'

Dina nodded through the tears. 'I promise.'

* * *

'He's here!' Dina announced excitedly to her classmates. They scrambled from their seats and gathered at the window to see Olympic champion Darren Campbell arrive at the gates of her secondary school, Newstead Wood. He was one of the four sprinters who'd won gold for Great Britain in the 4 x 100 metres relay race in Athens 2004; they were a dream team who had demonstrated just how technically brilliant the skill of baton passing could be. Dina couldn't believe it. She'd watched him run the second leg on the TV over four years earlier and now in 2008 he was here: an Olympic gold medallist visiting their school.

Darren was visiting on behalf of the Youth Sports Trust to announce a new partnership he'd founded with Olympic champion Todd Bennett, called the Team Superschools project. Together, they planned to visit over two thousand schools before the 2012 London Olympics to introduce children to the basics of athletics. Before they took on a variety of physical challenges and warm-ups in the school hall, Darren spoke to Dina's class.

He looked ordinary enough in a white sports T-shirt, but Dina's prepared questions for him soon disappeared from her mind as he grinned at the class and began to speak in a rich Mancunian accent.

'Who managed to watch any of the Beijing Olympic Games coverage this summer?'

'Me!' Everyone threw their hands up.

'And why's the next one so special?'

They all replied in unison: 'Because it's in London!'

'Our capital city!'

They all nodded.

'Did anyone see Jessica Ennis take bronze in the 100 metres hurdles last year at the European Championships in Hungary?'

Dina nodded her head vigorously. She loved the British athlete and was enjoying watching her career unfold.

'Anyone know what her time was?'

Dina stuck her hand up and shouted out: 'It was 13.1 seconds!'

Darren smiled broadly. 'Excellent! You must be a fan.'

'I am!'

'Well, she'll be wanting to beat that time at the next Olympics. And I think she's on track to take gold next time. Four years. Seems like a long time away, right?'

The class nodded.

'But the champions we will see at 2012 are all working towards it now. We just won't get to see how hard they're working. We won't see the failures, the false starts, the tears or disappointments and injuries, we'll just see the results of all the hard work they put in. I was lucky enough to train with my coach Linford Christie six days a week in the years leading up to our relay team's success in 2004. Without that hard work we wouldn't have beaten the American team. And in this game, split seconds count. We beat them by just 0.01 seconds in a season's best of 38.07 seconds.'

The Olympics did seem eons away to 12-year-old Dina too, but she knew that the work she was doing now with John was building up her strength and endurance for her own athletic goals. She'd progressed to Blackheath and Bromley and was now training for eight hours a week at their training ground.

From planks to push-ups and squats, Dina worked on slowly building up her core strength along with running sets of 100 metres at race pace with two-minute breaks in between. In the summer of 2009 she came second in the 100 metres at the Blackheath and Bromley Open at a personal best of 13.4 seconds. She wanted to shave at least a second off in time for the Kent Schools Championships the following summer.

As John explained to her, their aim was to concentrate on her personal bests rather than worry about always being the fastest in the race.

'We need to work towards you comfortably

beating your own targets,' he said, 'rather than focusing on who the fastest is in the race, the county or even the country. You don't have to be the best, but I do expect you to commit to being your best.'

As a budding athlete of the school, Dina was picked to show Darren around the school's track and field facilities later in the afternoon. Her nerves subsided a little and she began to share her hopes to compete in the European Championships one day. When Dina's mother came to collect her from school she was chatting away excitedly to the Olympic medallist.

As soon as she spotted her mum, Dina rushed over to her.

'Mum – could you take a photo of us?' She looked back at Darren and asked him: 'If that's okay?'

'Yes, of course!' Darren replied.

Darren had brought in his Olympic gold medal and asked Dina if she'd like to hold it.

She held the medal in her hands. 'It feels heavy!'

Darren laughed. 'I should think so, there's meant to be at least six grams of gold in it!'

Dina thought how wonderful it must be for him to keep something like that, as a continual reminder of his achievement. She hoped she could feel the weight of a gold medal around her neck one day. She held it up to the camera and smiled.

Then Darren asked her: 'Dina, would you like to wear it?' It was as if he'd read her mind.

Dina's eyes lit up. 'Really?'

'Of course!'

She went to put it around her neck, but her mother stepped forward quickly to stop her.

'Ah, no, the first medal Dina wears will be her own.'

Dina felt her cheeks flush. Trust Mum to tell an Olympic champion what to do.

'Mum...' she muttered under her breath.

Darren nodded his head in approval.

'No, your mum's right. I remember thinking something very similar when I was around your age. That's a good mindset to have.'

Dina smiled, although she was still a little embarrassed.

'Do you want to have your own medal, Dina?' asked Darren.

Without a moment's hesitation, she replied: 'Yes.'

Darren looked into her determined eyes. He could see she meant it.

He turned to Dina's mother.

'As part of the launch for the Youth Sports Trust,' he said, 'we're handing out grants to help young athletes. I think Dina should apply.'

Julie smiled as Darren turned back to Dina and said: 'Whatever your dreams are, believe in them, because they can come true.'

As soon as Dina got home, she began work on her grant application with her mother. Together, they went through the list of questions. Towards the end, Dina was asked to provide a short personal statement. She thought long and hard for a minute before answering: 'I don't have to be *the* best but

I'm determined to show up and be *my* best.'

A few weeks later, Dina and her parents had something to celebrate. She'd been awarded a bursary to help towards training gear, sportswear and equipment.

Dina was very happy. It felt great to know that some world champions believed she was worth the investment. She thought back to the words Darren had left her with: 'Whatever your dreams are, believe in them, because they can come true.'

A few weeks later, Dina injured her foot in a hockey match and had to stop playing any sport to rest and recover. She desperately missed keeping active, but it helped her decide on the sport she most wanted to concentrate on. Out of all of them, she missed running the most. She was determined, more than ever, to make it her main focus.

CHAPTER 8

RECORD-BREAKER

11 July 2009

It was a warm day for the Aviva English Schools Athletics Championships. Dina stood in lane three as she prepared for the Junior Girls 4 x 100 metres relay race and took in the sheer size of the Don Valley Stadium in Sheffield. She quashed the urge to break out into a Beyoncé dance routine to control her nerves – a trick which usually worked in the call-up room, much to John's bewilderment.

Don Valley was surely the largest stadium where she'd competed so far, and in one of the biggest competitions. Her team weren't just running for their school, they were running for their county, Kent, and were up against seven others that included Lancashire, Manchester and West Yorkshire.

Dina had had a lot of fun practising with her relay team. Georgina Middleton had been chosen to lead the race. Dina herself would tackle the longest back straight on the second, before passing to Sophie Ayre. Rhiannon Jones would take the last leg.

Dina thought of her parents in the crowd. She knew her mum would be videoing her performance from start to finish. Her times had got steadily faster throughout the year; from her 12.9-second 100 metres at the Kent Schools Championships in April, to 12.8 seconds a month later. She knew she could make a difference to the race.

She was getting better at controlling her nerves before each race. In fact, she rather enjoyed them. She remembered a word of advice that Darren Campbell had given them in the talk at school: 'You need the heartbeat. But you need to control it.'

She knew the nerves would be building in the rest of the team as they stood in their positions around the track, waiting for what felt like an eternity before the start. They'd practised their handovers as often as they possibly could but there was little time or funding to perfect them.

Dina felt a surge of excitement as she heard the muffled tones of the announcer over the tannoy. 'On your marks...'

She always thought of John's words – 'Don't hold the horses' – while she did her final few jumps to warm up and anticipated the start of the race.

'Get set...' Dina's heart raced as she waited for the gun to fire.

Bang!

They blasted out of the blocks. West Yorkshire started well and soon took the lead while Georgina trailed in fourth behind. Dina knew she and the rest of the Kent team had some catching up to do. As Georgina drew close, Dina began the run for the handover. Once she took the baton, she flew down the back straight, her legs pounding, staring determinedly ahead to Sophie, who held her hand out behind her. West Yorkshire were still in the lead but the changeover between Dina and Sophie was seamless.

'Go Sophie, go!' Dina cheered her on and watched with delight as she gained ground on the inside to overtake West Yorkshire and Norfolk. On the final bend she took the lead before she handed to Rhiannon, who raced down the final stretch.

Now Kent had the lead.

But it wasn't their time to take gold. In the last 10 metres, West Yorkshire and Norfolk closed in steadily on Rhiannon, leaving her to trail home in third place. However, the Kent team were happy to pick up bronze.

'Yay! We got a medal!'

Dina was hailed as the star of the team, who'd helped them claw back from fourth place on the second leg.

'I don't think we could have got ahead without

you, Dina.'

'You absolutely tore down that track.'

Dina protested, 'But, guys, it was a team effort!'

'You were born to sprint!'

That summer, the medals kept coming for Dina in her personal races. In August, she took gold in the 100 metres at the England Under 17 and Under 15 Championships at Bedford Stadium, the same month that she won the same event at the SEAA Under 15 and Under 20 Inter Counties Match in Watford.

Yet, despite these successes, Dina was a little frustrated that her times weren't improving significantly. They continued to hover around the 12.10 and 12.12 second mark and were slower than some of her earlier runs in the year.

She discussed her concern with John. 'I thought runners were meant to get faster in the summer!'

John reassured her. 'Sometimes this happens after a year of hard training. I know you want to be faster but if we push your body any harder we could cause too much stress on your muscles, which we don't want to do. It's important to pace yourself. Continue to do the work and the faster times will come.'

He added: 'Dina, right now, you're winning most of your races but that won't be the case when you start competing in bigger events. On the European or international stage it may take you time to pick up a medal; for now, you could be coming in fourth or fifth.'

The thought of coming fourth in any race seemed bizarre to Dina, but she trusted John and knew he always had her best interests at heart.

'If you want to be a champion,' he said, 'you need to be able to accept that and not give up. We go at the pace that's right for you, okay?'

She nodded.

Yet, in early August, Dina achieved a personal best of 39.16 seconds in the 300 metres at the Tonbridge Avril Bowring Open. It was a vast improvement on her time of 44.37 seconds earlier that year.

***

Dina flopped down in front of the TV and tucked into her favourite pepperoni pizza to celebrate. As she savoured each mouthful, she overheard her mother on the phone to John.

'The fastest what? Really?! That's amazing news! Thank you, John.'

A few seconds later she peered around the door of the lounge. 'Guess what, Dina? You're a record-breaker!'

'What?'

'No other 13-year-old has ever run that fast in a 300-metre race!'

'In the country?'

'In the world!'

Dina's mouth fell open.

'Isn't that fantastic?'

'Yes!'

Dina couldn't believe it. She was a record-breaker. And suddenly the thought of breaking more records seemed possible.

'I think this could be the first of many,' said her mother.

CHAPTER 9

HARD WORK PAYS OFF

'Head up! Chest up! Keep your knees bent!'

The autumn nights were drawing in and it was getting colder out on the track at Norman Park. John had increased her training to four times a week ahead of the English Schools' Championships the following summer. It was her dream to win the Championships in either the 100 or 200 metres with a new personal best. Her 200 was currently 25 seconds and they were both working on reducing that.

John began setting new exercises for Dina to improve her overall fitness, which included jumps, hops and skips. As Dina practised jumping up on to a bench in the gym, John explained why they were important.

'When you exert maximum force on your muscles in a short space of time, it will help to increase their power and strength.'

'You'd better be right, John,' Dina groaned, as she struggled to regain her breath after her fourth round of 10 jumps.

John smiled. 'I am. You'll be even more springy in no time.'

Dina sighed. She knew the workouts were important, but they weren't as much fun as just racing down the track. 'It's a bit boring, John. Can I listen to some music when I do it?' She loved to work out to Jay-Z.

John shook his head. 'It's important to maintain absolute focus when you do these exercises. If you get distracted you might use your muscles in the wrong way or do some damage.'

Dina was normally very tired when she returned

home from a long day of school and training. She was often tempted to flop out on the sofa and catch up on the latest reality TV show before bed. But she knew that wasn't an option now. She looked at the homework schedule she'd drawn up to help her juggle schoolwork and training.

Dina had also recently picked her GCSE subjects. She still loved history as much as she had in primary school and was looking forward to studying it in more detail.

After studying from half nine to ten for a maths test the next day, and downing a banana smoothie snack made by her mum, Dina settled down to bed. She was asleep the second her head hit the pillow. The next day she would follow the same routine all over again. It was a tough schedule to stick to throughout the whole of the winter, but she had a temporary break at Christmas, vegging out in front of the TV watching movies, eating ice cream and chicken drumsticks. She vowed to return to training in the new year, in preparation for the summer championships.

Dina's hard work would pay off. Throughout early 2010 she excelled, winning almost every single 100- and 200-metre race she entered. In June she won the 200 metres at the Kent Schools Championships in 24.73 seconds.

'You can run it faster than this,' said John.

'I know,' she said in frustration.

'Don't waste your time beating yourself up about it, though. Conserve as much energy as possible ahead of the English Schools' Championships. We've got another four weeks to work on it. So do your best to avoid any drama going on at school, relax, watch movies – and no over-exerting yourself with any dance routines!'

Dina laughed. 'But they help me let off steam!'

'We need that steam for the track!'

Dina continued to train hard but took off one or two days a week to catch up on movies and relax with friends. It was nearly the summer holidays and classes were winding down a little after their end-of-year exams. One evening, she came to training in a more subdued mood than usual.

'What's up?' asked John, not used to seeing her like this.

'Has something happened at school?'

She shook her head.

'No, I just watched *The Notebook*! Oh John, it's so sad.' Her eyes began to well up.

'Oh no!' said John. 'When I said "Relax and watch movies" maybe I should have specified... don't watch anything that's going to upset you! You need all the energy you can get! From now on – no more tearjerkers! And definitely no scary movies!'

CHAPTER 10

A RISING STAR

9 July 2010

It was another warm July day and the final of the 200 metres at the next Aviva English Schools Championships, this time in Birmingham. Dina was both nervous and excited as she took in the size of the Alexander Stadium. All her races throughout the year had built up to this and she couldn't wait to fly down the track.

She felt like a rocket waiting for lift-off as she stretched and jumped up and down on the spot to warm up her muscles. She'd won the heat earlier that day in a time of 25 seconds, but she wanted to beat that – so John's theory seemed to have worked. She thought of him in the crowd, watching with her parents. She knew they got just as nervous as she did before a race, but there was nothing they could do to help as they watched from the stands. In the end, it was always down to her to run the race well.

She glanced briefly at the other competitors. She remembered John's warning. 'Never become complacent enough to think that you're the best because anything can happen in athletics. Don't give someone the chance to be better than you.'

She looked down at the shoes her mum had recently bought her to replace the pair she purchased when she received her sports grant. That felt like a long time ago now. She smiled again as a shot of excitement ran through her. She wasn't going to let them down.

'On your marks...'

Dina jumped up and down one last time as she settled into the starting blocks.

'Get set...'

Bang!

It was a good start for Dina and she used the bend to her advantage to take the lead. The noise of the crowd blended into the background as she focused on lifting her knees and legs as high as she could, speeding down the last 60 metres. No one had a chance to close in on her as she flew out in front, her arms outstretched as she crossed the finishing line. A huge smile broke out on to her face as she checked her time on the clock: 24.93 seconds. She'd won. But more importantly, she'd beaten her previous personal best.

A month later, Dina won a gold medal in the 100 metres at the Aviva England Athletics Championships in Bedford. She ran a personal best of 12.00 seconds, beating her previous time of 12.21 seconds in an event two months earlier. Dina's confidence was growing all the time and she felt even more ready to take on international events.

As the summer drew to a close, John discussed

upcoming events with her. 'I think you're ready to compete at the next European Youth Olympics. How'd you like to go to Turkey next year?'

Dina's face lit up as she heard the word 'Olympics'.

'Oh, John, I'd love to!'

'Great.'

'Hang on, does that mean...?'

'Yes, you'll be representing Great Britain. This will be your first British vest!'

Dina pictured herself holding up the Union Jack as she ran the lap of honour. Her heart skipped a beat at the thought of running for her country. She was another step closer to becoming an Olympic champion.

***

The following summer, 2011, in Turkey, Dina once more thought of that vision of herself, draped in the Union Jack, in her mind as she settled into the blocks. She stared down the track two metres ahead of her and focused her mind. She was about to run in the final of the 200 metres at the European Youth Olympics. She'd performed well in the last two heats, coming in first and second place to qualify. In under 30 seconds' time, would she win a medal for Britain? Silence descended upon the Hüseyin Avni Aker Stadium.

'Set!' Dina put her head down, straightened her back and raised her body. She held her breath as she waited for the gun.

Bang!

Dina sprang out of the blocks but ran to a crashing halt when two shots were fired into the air. All the runners looked around accusingly at each other. One of them must have made a false start. Dina felt her cheeks grow hotter and her hands start to sweat as the event adjudicator walked towards her with a stern expression on their face. She felt a deep sense of shame in the pit of her stomach as she realised she was the one who had made a mistake. As her cheeks grew hotter, she began to walk off the track, and back towards the athletes' call-up room. She felt someone pat her on the shoulder and gently say her name.

'Dina, are you okay?' It was Jo Jennings, the former English high-jump champion, who was also development manager for British Athletics.

'I'm fine,' replied Dina. She did her best to keep her head held high, although she knew she was on the verge of tears.

'Don't cry here,' she told herself.

As she entered the call-up room she looked at the concerned faces of John and her parents, who ran over to comfort her.

'I'm sorry!' she said, before she burst into floods of tears. She felt absolutely devastated. The heats had gone so well but she'd ruined her chances of becoming a champion in a split second.

'There, there,' said John, 'you won't be the first or last athlete to make a false start. Happens to the best of them – even Linford Christie, wouldn't you know?'

Dina tried to get her words out through her tears. 'I can't believe it, I've failed – failed!'

'Dina, you are human. You will make mistakes sometimes, I'm afraid.'

'But I don't want to make mistakes!'

'It's part of this process. This one mistake today will mean you'll probably never make another false start again in your life.'

'You think so?'

'Yes. You will improve because of this. You will become a better runner. I know it.'

The uncomfortable sensation began to ease in Dina's stomach a little. She'd had John as her coach long enough to know she could trust him.

John continued. 'You need to take away the positives from today. Number one, you're good enough to compete internationally. Number two, you've beaten your personal best in the 200 metres. And number three, most importantly of all, your mascara hasn't run.'

Dina mustered a smile. She'd got into the habit of applying eye make-up before each of her runs, obstinately telling John: 'I like make-up. Besides, I want to look ready for the cameras if I win a race.' The plaits were long gone too, replaced with a more mature and sleek bun.

Dina felt awful but she knew deep down that John was right. Something good would come from this.

'This is part of the process,' John had told her, 'of going from junior to senior. I know you've got it in you to make that jump.'

Dina vowed there and then to keep going and to work on her starts out of the blocks to ensure she never made another false start again. On the flight back home, she was already looking ahead to 2012. It was going to be an important year. Not just for London, when all eyes of the world would be on the city, but for Dina, who would be sitting her GCSEs and training to compete in the World Junior Athletics Championships.

CHAPTER 11

THE END OF AN ERA

Dina and her friends raced to the top of Poverest Park. They'd just taken their last GCSE exam and were thrilled to be out of hot and stuffy exam rooms for good. Temperatures across the country had been soaring.

They all shouted at the top of their lungs: 'No more exams!'

They proceeded to roll back down the hill laughing and giggling, just like they had when they were kids. This was going to be a special summer. Not just because they'd finished their GCSEs but because London was hosting the Summer

77

Olympics. The 2012 logo was emblazoned across posters and billboards across Orpington, and the capital's other surrounding towns and boroughs, along with the faces of the sporting heroes the country was pinning their hopes on: Jessica Ennis, Mo Farah, Greg Rutherford. The event that Darren Campbell had talked about so excitedly, all those years ago in her school classroom, was finally upon them.

Dina knew, though, that she couldn't switch off completely over that summer. While her friends talked excitedly about the upcoming school prom, where they were going on holiday and how they planned to celebrate, her mind kept drifting off to what was ahead of her. Within a month she'd be in Barcelona. Not for a holiday, not for relaxation – but to compete in the World Junior Athletics Championships.

She sighed as she saw her friends tuck into their second tub of ice cream each, and said, 'It's torture to watch you eat that.'

'Can't you just have a bit?'

'It wouldn't just be a bit. Anyway, I promised John. And he told me I can have as much as I want – after I've won a medal! I'm telling you now, the afternoon of the fifteenth of July... I've got a date with a whole vanload of the stuff, I don't care what he says!'

They all laughed.

'You've got such discipline, Dina, I couldn't stick to it.'

'Yeah, it's worth it.'

'You'll smash it, Dina.'

'Well, that's not very likely,' said Dina. 'I'm competing on a world stage. I'm up against some great runners from the USA and Jamaica. For once, I think I'll be watching their backsides fly ahead of me.'

'You could get a medal for modesty, Dina.'

'No, honestly, if I do well enough in the 200 metre heats to qualify for the finals, I'll be really happy. And beat my personal best, of course.'

'What do you need to get to achieve that?'

'Shave off at least a second.'

'Just a second?'

Dina laughed. 'Remember, Kelly Holmes won by one five hundreth of a second. Seconds don't count in a race, hundreths of a second count!'

'You're up there with the best of them Dina, that's what counts.'

She smiled. 'We'll see.'

CHAPTER 12

PERSONAL
BEST

13 July 2012

Dina took one last look around the Estadi Olímpic Lluís Companys stadium in Barcelona as she prepared for the 200 metres final. This was the stadium where the 1992 Olympics had taken place, three years before she was even born. She was standing on the same track where champions Steve Redgrave and Linford Christie had wowed the world with their outstanding performances. She gave herself a moment to take it all in.

In comparison, how important was her run? She shook her head and smiled. Hadn't Allyson Felix, a runner she'd admired for years, broken a record in these Championships eight years before?

No – Dina reasoned that she might not be an elite champion just yet, but she was heading in the right direction and about to achieve something incredible in her own right, if she could focus and get a handle on the butterflies churning in her stomach.

She had performed outstandingly in the 200 metres qualifiers earlier in the day, bringing in times that improved with each heat: from 23.71 seconds down to 23.57 seconds. These times were currently not that far behind the USA's Dezerea Bryant at 23.11 or the Bahamas' Anthonique Strachan at 23.28.

The gun fired and the athletes tore off down the track. It was clear from the start that Anthonique had made an incredible start, exploding out of the blocks like a bullet, with Dezerea and Olivia Ekpone of the USA hot on her heels. Dina concentrated on running as fast as she could but she couldn't catch up with them and trailed behind, something that was still so new to her. She saw Anthonique cross the finishing line to win a record-breaking gold at 22.53 seconds. Olivia and Dezerea followed neck-and-neck behind her to take silver and bronze.

Dina crossed the line in seventh place but as she checked the clock her heart skipped a beat. Despite her placing, she'd achieved a new personal best: 23.50.

'Yes!' She punched the air with her fists and threw her hands up to her face as relief washed over her.

'Well done, Dina.' She heard John's calm voice behind her. He was never one to get carried away with emotion. She glanced over at the British runner Desirèe Henry who'd come in fourth. Dina knew she'd be disappointed, just as she was, not to win a place on the podium. But, deep down, Dina knew that if she kept working on improving her times, one day she would.

Dina was taken aback when the press began

to gather around her and fire questions. She was beginning to look like a hot new sporting hope for Britain.

'With a performance like that, Dina, do you feel hopeful for the European Junior Championships next year?'

Dina smiled politely and nodded. 'Yes, I'm looking forward to them.'

But in all honesty, there was only one thing on her mind right then.

She turned to John. 'I'd kill for some ice cream!'

'Yeah, I think you deserve it.'

The taste of vanilla ice cream melting in her mouth had never felt so good. She was elated. She had made the 200 metres final and achieved a new PB.

CHAPTER 13

LONDON 2012

Dina felt the hairs on the back of her neck go up as she entered the Olympic Stadium. The sound of 80,000 excited and expectant home crowd fans echoed around the arena. In every direction that Dina looked there was a sign or banner in support of the British athletes performing that day.

It was Saturday, 4 August 2012 and Dina, along with her friend Shannon and other athletes from Blackheath and Bromley, had all been chosen to be box carriers, which meant they had the job of carrying kit for the competing British Olympic athletes. Initially, Dina had been disappointed she wasn't chosen for the following day, when Usain Bolt was running. But, already, they could sense they were about to witness something magical that day.

As Dina made her way to the call-up room with the other volunteers, her hands began to tremble slightly. She knew she had to focus on her job but it was difficult not to get distracted.

'I can't believe it!' Shannon hissed under her breath. 'I'm carrying Mo Farah's shorts! He could become an Olympic champion in these today!'

She looked at Dina, who started giggling.

'Dina, I'm serious. I'm not sure I can do it! What if I get so overwhelmed I faint and drop his box?!'

'You'd better let me carry it then, if you're not up to the job!'

'No way!' They began to squabble over who should be tasked with this great honour.

But as they walked into the call-up room, they felt not only the weight of the boxes they carried but the weight of pressure and responsibility each athlete was feeling.

Dina was glad that John had chosen her to volunteer. This was a great opportunity to see and feel what it was like to compete on a world stage, as well as to experience the added pressure of performing to a home crowd, who so desperately wanted you to win.

The tension was almost unbearable. Despite the din awaiting them outside, there was barely any sound in the room as the athletes paced up and down, warmed up their muscles or spoke in muffled tones to their coaches, whose expressions gave away little of their own feelings.

Darren's words from four years earlier returned to Dina as she watched Mo Farah, Greg Rutherford and Jessica Ennis prepare for the biggest challenges of their careers to date. Few of the spectators would know of the struggles or pains they'd overcome to reach that competitive level. Nor could they comprehend just how nervous they were.

This was a revelation for Dina. Here she was,

just a few feet from some of the most talented athletes in the world, athletes who were probably about to make Olympic history. Yet even these revered sporting heroes got nervous. It reassured her somehow. Yes, she thought, everyone gets nervous. But it's about how you work with your nerves, rather than allowing them to control you. She thought about the races she had run and each race she would run in the future. She vowed to herself there and then: 'Rather than battling my own nerves, I'll accept they'll always exist and work with them to propel me forward.'

At the edge of the track, Dina was close enough to watch a series of emotions cross Jessica's face as she waited to run the 800 metres, her final event, in lane eight; emotions of doubt, anxiety, dread and fear. They were all there. Dina couldn't imagine the pressure she was feeling in that moment. She was in first place in the heptathlon event, but the gold medal rested on her performance in the 800 metres. Jess knew that if she ran it in a time that was close to her best, no other runner could catch her. In second place was the Lithuanian athlete Austra Skujytė, but this race wasn't Austra's strongest event. Could the Ukraine's Lyudmyla Yosypenko cover enough ground to catch her?

Dina gripped the hands of her fellow box carriers as they all held their breath and watched from the side of track eight, waiting for the gun to fire. Could the World Champion take gold for her country in front of a home crowd? Jess got a good start out of the blocks and comfortably took the lead in the first 400-metre lap. It looked as though she had the race wrapped up. As the bell for the final lap rang Dina felt Shannon's grip on her arm tighten. Jess was still in the lead. But then, in the final 300 metres, she faced fresh challenges as three competitors passed her – one included Tatyana Chernova. Dina and the other volunteers began to pace up and down to work off their nervous energy.

Dina could hardly bear to watch as the support from the crowd reached new heights, with cries of 'Come on, Jess!' and 'Bring it back!' The entire stadium was cheering Jess on to win, helping to provide the energy she needed to fight the last part of this battle.

They watched in amazement as Jess turned the corner of the final lap and clawed her way back. With a sudden burst of speed, she overtook the athletes ahead of her and took on the home straight. The noise of the crowd was almost deafening as she took a clear lead. No one could get close to her now. Victory was in sight. She crossed the line and stretched out her arms before she fell to the ground and allowed her tears to flow. The crowd erupted.

Celebrating with her friends on the sidelines, Dina could feel the sense of joy and pride sweep around the stadium. They all knew how much it meant to Jess to win. Her disappointment at Beijing in 2008 and the injuries that had held her back all melted away in that moment. She'd overcome them all to succeed. It was her destiny to take gold that Saturday in front of an 80,000-strong home crowd who could share in that victory.

Suddenly, Dina's own destiny seemed clear to her, as the celebrations continued to reverberate around the stadium and indeed, the entire city of London. Dina was inspired, not only by Jess's physical strength but her determination to overcome her nerves and do battle with the doubt and uncertainty in her mind. She felt certain that she could incite the same feelings of joy and pride in people too. Just from running in a straight line. She laughed for a moment at the simplicity of it all. But there was a deep sense of certainty within her that this was what she wanted to do.

Jess struggled to hold back the tears on the podium as she collected her gold medal – the first athletics gold of the 2012 Olympics for Great Britain – and held it up to the roaring crowd. Afterwards, she wrapped herself in the Olympic Champion flag and an interviewer asked her how she felt. Dina watched as a huge smile broke out over her face when she answered: 'It just doesn't feel real.

To have all this support and to win in London is incredible.'

But the celebrations for Great Britain were not over yet. Dina watched from the sidelines again while a huge cheer went up for Mo Farah. He was the hot favourite to win the 10,000-metre race but with 25 laps to run and 27 other athletes competing, everyone knew it would be no mean feat. Ten minutes in, and with eighteen laps to go, Shannon joined Dina to watch his progress.

'Where is he?' They both scanned the track for his dark blue shorts.

'There he is!'

'He's really far behind!' Shannon groaned.

'It's early days,' said Dina. She knew from her cross-country days that he was pacing. 'He's got time to move in for the attack yet.'

Dina's words proved to be right. They watched, spellbound, as Mo started to move slowly and surely up the field.

'He's getting into position!' Dina shouted. The

excited roars from the crowd showed no signs of abating. They had energy enough for Mo too. Twenty minutes in and Mo was in seventh place with the USA's Galen Rupp and Ethiopia's Kenenisa Bekele steaming ahead.

But Dina knew all the athletes would have to look out for the Farah sprint.

'Look!' cried Dina as they watched him steadily move in on the attack. 'He's chasing Bekele!'

Then, with four laps to go, they watched Mo take the lead for the first time.

Dina and Shannon jumped up and down in excitement. But his fight was far from over as the other athletes continued to challenge and take the lead. With just over one lap to go, the runners bunched together, and everyone waited with bated breath. Who would make the first move to break free?

Then, as the bell rang for the final lap, they saw Mo take the lead, breaking into a long sprint. Bekele and Rupp were hot on his heels, but they were clearly struggling to keep up with him as he continued to increase his lead on the home straight. Could he take another gold medal for Britain that day?

'He's done it!' Dina and Shannon leapt up and down as they watched him cross the finish line and fall to the ground and kiss it.

What a night for Britain! Tears of pride ran down Dina's face as she watched Mo's overjoyed wife and daughter make their way down from the crowd to celebrate with him.

It wasn't the last British win of the day though. Greg Rutherford leapt 8.1 metres to take gold in the long jump. What an unbelievable day.

The news of Britain's success was splashed across the papers the next morning. The overjoyed faces of the Olympic champions were emblazoned across the front pages, along with the headline: 'Super Saturday'. Dina couldn't believe she'd been a part of one of the greatest days in British sporting history. She knew it had changed her life forever.

A few weeks later Dina had another reason to celebrate. But it had nothing to do with sport.

'Just tell me I've passed!' Dina covered her eyes while her mum logged onto the school system to find out Dina's exam results.

'Darling, you've done more than pass.'

Dina uncovered her eyes. 'You've got 10 A*s!'

Dina leapt around for joy. It was the perfect way to end a magical summer. She was heading into the sixth form to study A-levels in Biology, History and Politics.

CHAPTER 14

TRAINING HARD

Dina and Shannon danced around the kitchen, singing along to a Jay-Z song. It was the last day of the Christmas holidays and they were relaxing before the hard work resumed back at school and in training; Shannon was now also coached by John.

Dina sighed at the thought of returning to the hard grind. She'd been used to juggling schoolwork and training for years, but the pace had gone up a gear in the last term. As well as adjusting to A-levels, she was training for the European Athletics Junior Championships in Italy in Summer 2013. After her time off, she felt sluggish and demotivated.

She told her mum: 'This is the problem with winter. I love Christmas but I dread going back out on the track again after time off. I'll have slowed down like a right tortoise, I bet you!'

Dina had the London Under 20/Senior Games coming up at Lee Valley and admitted that she was a bit concerned about the 60-metre race she was running at the end of January.

Her mum knew she always strove to beat her personal bests, but she could see she wasn't her usual, energetic self.

'Dina, I think you need an incentive.'

Dina's ears pricked up. 'Oh yeah?'

'What was your last PB on the 60 metres?'

'7.48 seconds.'

Dina had run it at Crystal Palace the month before.

'Okay, if you get that down to 7.40 seconds by the end of January, I'll buy you a phone.'

Dina's eyes lit up. She loved a challenge and

needed one most during the long dark days in January.

'Mum, you're on!'

They shook hands on the bet.

From 7.48 to 7.40 seconds? Surely it was possible? She thought of the great Usain Bolt, who could cover 20 metres in just 1.61 seconds, and she smiled. It still amazed her the difference each hundredth of a second could make.

A few weeks after the race at Lee Valley, Dina arrived home to find a gift waiting for her on the kitchen table. She beamed. She knew exactly what it was. She'd won the 60 metres in a new personal best of 7.36, beating the time she'd originally set with her mum. Her local paper interviewed her for a piece highlighting the challenges of clocking incredible speeds while still tackling schoolwork and training.

It felt like another turning point for Dina. Since the 2012 Olympics, she had begun to feel that a career in athletics was not just highly likely but inevitable, and was looking ahead to the next Summer Olympics in 2016.

She told the press: 'I've got my heart set on Rio now. If you'd asked me a year ago, I don't think I would have believed it was possible. But I'm taking it more seriously now.'

She spent up to eight hours a week on the track with John, who could see that she wasn't taking the responsibility of being one of Britain's top sprinters lightly.

'If I relax,' she said, 'I give someone else the chance to beat me, John. You've always said that athletics is a sport where anyone can come out of nowhere.'

But history, particularly modern history, was still a strong passion of hers and she continued to work hard throughout the first year of her A-levels. While she trained with John, she would reel off fascinating facts about the European dictators during World War Two before rushing home to finish an essay on them.

As John would watch her leave, he often wondered how she maintained the stamina to juggle both athletics and her studies. But he knew that the standards Dina set herself in both areas were equally high. Success in one field often seeped into the other. Her confidence at school increased when she exceeded targets on the track.

As she worked towards completing her mock exams that summer, she continued to beat her personal bests. On 6 July in Birmingham she won the English Schools Championships 200 metres in a time of 23.63 seconds, despite racing into a strong headwind on the home straight.

John told her: 'Keep going like this, Dina, and you'll fly at the Junior Championships.'

Dina looked at him, bemused. It wasn't like John to praise her in this way. But she knew they both felt confident she could beat her personal best again in Italy.

Dina was extremely excited about Italy for a number of reasons. Not only did she have the opportunity to compete against some of Europe's fastest athletes but she was taking part in the 4 x 100 metres relay with three other athletes from Great Britain: Desirèe Henry, Yasmin Miller and Steffi Wilson. She always enjoyed relays because they were a chance to work on the same team with runners she admired and so often competed against.

Dina and Desirèe had become good friends during their practice for the relay, so Dina knew they'd both be grateful their relay took place after the sprints. However, any uncomfortable feelings about competing against her friend disappeared as she laid eyes on the small town of Reiti where the Championships took place. For a moment, she was too distracted by Romanesque churches and turreted houses perched upon snow-capped mountains. It occurred to her how fortunate she was to visit such beautiful European cities because of sport.

The day of the final for the 200 metres arrived. Dina was hopeful she could beat her personal best despite the heat in the stadium. 'Keep your personal best in mind and the rest will follow,' John always said. She would come first in the heats, but she knew she still faced stiff competition from Desirèe and Tessa van Schagen, who weren't far behind her with their own personal bests. It would be a close race.

Tackling the bend was often the trickiest part of the race for Dina, because she tended to tighten up on it, and so she remembered the techniques she'd worked on with John: 'Tilt your head and the hips and shoulders will follow. Don't raise or straighten the head until you reach the straightaway. And never burn the turn!'

As Dina settled into the starting blocks she felt ready to spring out of them fast. She was getting better at conserving her energy before each race and using her nerves to propel her forward.

The gun fired.

Dina flew out of the blocks like a bullet. She eased into the bend effortlessly. As she approached the home straight, she told herself: 'That was a good turn, you can relax into the race from here.' She crossed the finish line to take first place in a personal best of 23.29 seconds, with Desirèe and Tessa finishing second and third respectively.

As the press clamoured to talk to her, Dina was still out of breath. At 17, she was the world's youngest medallist at a world athletics championships for 20 years. She had enough energy to smile and answer questions though.

After the ceremony, Dina and Desirèe hugged each other and clutched their gold and silver medals close to their chests. Yasmin and Steffi came running over to congratulate them.

'That was amazing!' they cried. 'You can't relax just yet, though!'

Dina and Desirèe looked at each other.

'No way! We've got a race to win tomorrow!'

Dina couldn't wait to run with the team the next day and had difficulty sleeping that night, as she ran over the events of the day in her head. She'd won a gold medal. Could she win another tomorrow?

It rained the following morning. The team sighed with relief that the air around the stadium had cooled as they walked out to the track. Dina took her place on the second leg; the longest stretch to run. She thought of Yasmin at the start, who she knew was nervous.

'I hope the baton won't be so wet from my sweat that I'll drop it!'

Dina reassured her. 'Don't worry, it'll all be over before you know it!'

They'd achieved a great time in the heats, but all of them wanted to break it.

A huge cheer from the crowd went up as the gun fired for the start of the race. Yasmin made good headway on the turn and sprinted towards Dina, who prepared to take the baton from her. After a seamless handover she pelted down the longest stretch towards Steffi, taking the lead and clearing at least two feet in the race. After she handed to

Steffi, she watched her pelt down the track towards Desirèe for the home straight. It was looking close. Déborah Sananes of France and Eefje Boons of the Netherlands were almost neck-and-neck with Desirèe.

'Come on Desirèe!' The team screamed at the top of their lungs as they watched her pound towards the finish line, determined to see off her challengers. When she crossed the line first, the three of them ran over to her laughing and crying, 'You did it! You did it!'

They leapt up and down as they checked their time on the board.

'43.81 seconds!' they all screamed in unison.

Not only had they won gold, but they'd also broken the UK junior record. Dina couldn't believe what an incredible year 2013 had been – and it wasn't over yet by any means.

CHAPTER 15

A HUGE OPPORTUNITY

Despite her successes in Italy, the athletics season wasn't over yet for Dina. As a result of her relay win, she was asked to run in the senior relay team at the 2013 London Anniversary Games.

Dina was thrilled not only return to the Olympic Stadium, but to help the team – consisting of Anyika Onuora, Annabelle Lewis and Ashleigh Nelson – take gold in 42.69 seconds, the fastest women's relay time in 12 years. This time she had been the first runner in the relay and it had caught the eye of the British selectors deciding the final line-up for the World Championships in Moscow the following month. One afternoon in the gym, Dina answered her phone. It was the coach Rana Reider.

'Oh, hi Rana,' said Dina nonchalantly.

'How would you like to come to Moscow with me?'

Dina couldn't believe her ears.

'What? Did you just say...?'

'Yes Dina, we'd like you to run in the 4 x 100 relay.'

Dina could hardly get her response out. At seventeen, she was still so young, yet they had faith in her.

'Are you kidding?'

Rana's reply was simple: 'Dina, we believe you can do this.'

'Thank you! Thank you for this opportunity!'

She knew this was a great opportunity to improve. She was no longer running against Europeans or juniors. She was competing against world champions.

However, she felt herself quivering a little when

she realised she'd be running against gold medallist and Olympic champion Shelly-Ann Fraser-Pryce in the relay. After her performances at London 2012, Shelly-Ann had been lauded as 'the greatest female sprinter of all time'.

John offered Dina some advice. 'Be inspired by her but don't be intimidated by her. Respect her but don't idolise her. Otherwise, you'll panic and lose concentration when you run.'

Dina nodded.

'You have just as much right to be there as they do,' added John. 'And this will help you to make the important transition from junior to senior.'

Dina laughed. 'I'll do my best to just think of her as a normal person.'

'She's not a superhero! Remember how nervous Mo Farah and Jess were? No doubt she'll be going through it too. Just concentrate on yourself.'

'Thanks, John.'

'And, remember, you're the youngest athlete to be selected for the Great Britain and Northern

Ireland Squad in these Championships.'

Dina smiled. As the least experienced in big championships, she'd been put on to start for the relay. She knew she'd benefit from her new team's combined extra years of track experience. Ashleigh Nelson, Annabelle Lewis and Hayley Jones all had personal bests that Dina knew would fare them well if they reached the final.

But as she took her starting place on lane three for the final, on a blazing hot afternoon at Luzhniki Stadium, her nerves kicked in. She stepped from side to side and tapped the baton nervously against her leg until she caught sight of her face on the screen, looking serious with her two side plaits tied back into a ponytail. She broke out into a smile, in an attempt to contradict how nervous she felt, and waved to the camera as a large cheer went up for her.

'Wow,' she said to herself. 'People are watching me run.' She'd never been in a position where she felt such a weight of responsibility. A feeling of horror went through her as she thought, 'The papers will hate me if I mess up! And I can't let my teammates down!' Their careers and aspirations were on the line too.

Great Britain's team had won the heat two hours earlier that afternoon in 42.75 seconds. But now they were running against the superb Jamaican and USA teams. Shelly-Ann Fraser-Pryce, for Jamaica, was standing on the very same track as Dina, waiting to take on the home stretch in the anchor leg. Dina had watched her take gold in the 100 and 200 metres in record times just a week before.

Just when Dina realised her negative thinking was beginning to spiral out of control, she remembered John's words: 'Respect her. Don't idolise her.'

She smiled as she thought of the Greek heroes she loved studying at school. She remembered the wreath she had drawn on her picture of Kelly Holmes' head. 'Come on Dina, focus, you can do this. Do a great start for your team.'

'On your marks...'

Dina felt the sweat seep through to the baton she was holding in her hand while the announcer said the words they were all waiting for. One last cheer went up from the crowd and then there was silence.

Dina took one last jump up and down before she settled into the blocks.

'Get set!'

Bang!

Dina flew out of the blocks and round the bend towards Ashleigh for the first handover. The change happened fast, and she watched with relief as Ashleigh tore off down the straight. But it was clearly Jamaica's race. Dina watched in awe as Shelly-Ann hared it down the last leg with a clear eight-metre lead, her pink strip of hair flying behind her. She looked for Hayley, who appeared to have been swallowed up by France and the USA, who took silver and bronze. Dina shook hands with the other competitors before she ran over to her teammates to celebrate.

'Great race, guys!'

Although they'd failed to make a place for Great Britain on the podium, they knew fourth place was not be sniffed at. They'd been up against some of the best teams in the world. And Dina was delighted to see Shelly-Ann run that fast in a record-winning race of 41.29 seconds, matching Usain Bolt's success and taking three medals at the Championships.

However, the team had news for her.

'We're going to contest it – we think France made an illegal changeover.'

They all watched Jamaica, France and the USA claim their medals, but after the ceremony their protest was upheld and the French team were disqualified. The girls jumped around for joy as they received confirmation of their bronze medal.

'I can't believe it!' Dina cried down the phone to her parents, who were watching the games back in England.

'You've done your country proud,' her mum replied.

She had. But Dina's bronze medal was also proof that she could compete on a world stage.

To cap an extraordinary 2013, just weeks before her eighteenth birthday, she was shortlisted for the BBC Young Sports Personality of the Year. She felt more ready than ever to make the move from junior to senior, and looked ahead with great anticipation to her first professional senior championships in Zurich the following year.

CHAPTER 16

WORLD JUNIOR CHAMPIONSHIPS

Dina and John stepped up her training at the beginning of 2014, with a view to qualifying for Zurich in August. Before that, she was also competing in the World Junior Championships in Eugene, Oregon.

'We'll focus on increasing your speed and performance, as always,' said John, 'and keep you in good shape – and if you do well in Eugene, you're a definite contender.'

He smiled, and added: 'It means you might have to spend less time in the nail bar, though.'

Dina laughed. 'No way, John, I'm putting my

foot down. It's become a tradition now.'

It was true. Before every important run, Dina visited the nail bar for an elaborate new design, from multi-coloured roses to hearts and geometric symbols. It was also a welcome distraction from studying hard for the final year of her A-levels.

The summer of 2014 would be a gruelling one for Dina, in terms of studying and training; at one point she had to manage a schedule for both her A-level Biology exam and her trials for the World Junior Championships in Oregon. She continued to run some great races throughout the season, racing the 200 metres at Bedford in 22.74 seconds and the 100 metres at Loughborough International in 11.20.

One afternoon, when Dina and John were looking over schedules, they realised Dina would find out her A-level results on the same day she would be running the heats for the 200 metres in Zurich.

John said: 'You'd better make sure you get what

you want then – we don't want that putting you off the race!'

Dina had her heart set on studying History at King's College in London and needed three A grades to get in.

It was hard to manage such a schedule of both training and studying, but that summer she received an endorsement that spurred her on even further.

One afternoon, she turned up to training to find a pile of Nike clothing waiting for her in the dressing room.

'What's all this?' she said to John. 'You been on a shopping spree?'

'It seems Nike would like to sponsor you.'

'What?'

'Good thing you already like their sportswear, eh?'

Dina beamed from ear to ear. They looked at each other. Although John was laidback about the news, the gravitas wasn't lost on either of them. She was now a professional getting paid to do what she loved.

'I guess it's not just my parents who believe in me now!'

She kept this at the forefront of her mind as she prepared for the 100 metres at the World Junior Championships in Eugene. She thought back on the last two years as she stared down the track. She'd won the heats the day before, she just needed to make sure her time didn't drop too much.

She said to herself: 'Dina, you've faced tougher races than this and succeeded. And you weren't running as fast as you are now back then. You can do this.'

'On your marks, get set...'

Bang!

She knew she'd made a great start as she sprang out of the blocks and raced down the straight, taking a comfortable lead against Ecuador's Ángela Tenorio and the USA's Kaylin Whitney. When she crossed the finish line, she threw her hands up in the air as she heard the crowd cheer. Her time was 11.23 seconds! The words flashed up on the screen:

'Dina Asher-Smith: World Junior Champion!' She struggled to hold back her emotions, as she hugged and congratulated the other athletes on their run, including Desirèe who'd come in fourth.

As the sun dipped in the stadium, Dina wrapped herself in the British flag and chatted excitedly to reporters.

'What are your hopes and dreams for the future?' they asked.

'I can't even think right now – I'm just over the moon to have won!'

Her first senior competition in Zurich was less than a month away. Could she repeat her triumph in her first senior competition?

CHAPTER 17

A NERVOUS WAIT

Dina watched the sun sparkle on the clear blue waters of Lake Zurich as the coach rounded the streets towards Letzigrund Stadium. It was a beautiful day and, as much as she tried to distract herself with the sights of the city, her stomach was churning. It was the morning of her A-level results and she wished she could be back in London with her parents. She kept desperately trying to log on to her school's system to collect them but couldn't get any internet connection on her phone. She wanted to know those results before she started warming up for the 200 metres heats that day.

On the coach her fellow British athletes Jodie Williams and Bianca Williams tried to reassure her.

'You'll smash those A-levels, Dina!' said Bianca.

'And the heats!' Jodie agreed. 'We're both shaking with nerves at the thought of facing you in the final!'

At 20 years old, Bianca and Jodie were both a couple of years older than Dina and were more experienced athletes who'd won at the Commonwealth Championships. Dina felt very proud to have the opportunity to run against them. She'd seen Jodie pull a hamstring back in 2012 at the Olympic trials so she was pleased to see her back in shape now.

'Thanks, guys,' she said with a smile.

The coach neared the stadium. 'Ah well,' thought Dina, 'I'll just have to be patient and put it out of my mind.'

Suddenly, her phone beeped. It was a message from her mum. She had to double blink a few times to check she'd read it correctly: 'Three A's! Well done! Huge love, mum xx.'

'OMG!' Dina shouted out before texting back frantically: 'Are you sure?'

'Yes, I've just logged onto your account,' came the reply.

Jodie and Bianca patted her on the back. 'Good news then?'

Relief washed over Dina. 'I can't believe it! I'm going to King's! This is the best morning of my life!'

It was about to get even better. Later that morning she won the first round of heats in the 200 metres in 22.65 seconds.

But despite her great performance, Dina would still be denied her place in the final the next day. Just beforehand, while she warmed up in lane six, she took a final look down at her purple and yellow Nike trainers and felt a twinge in her hamstring. She put it out of her mind as a roar from the crowd went up for her, the youngest athlete in the race. But, when she propelled out of the blocks and approached the first bend, she felt the pain grow sharper.

'Ouch!' she cried out. She remembered John's warning about pushing her body too far. She slowed down and pulled over to the side, and watched Jodie win silver and the Netherlands' Dafne Schippers take gold.

Dina's summer of athletics may have been over, but at least she had a new academic year to look forward to at King's.

***

Dina's mum put her head round the door of her daughter's bedroom.

'Is that Duke I can hear?'

Dina looked up and nodded. She was busy revising for end-of-term exams.

'Bit different to the tempo I normally hear coming out of your bedroom.'

Dina laughed.

'I find some jazz a lot more relaxing for studying. I'll keep Jay-Z for warm-ups though! I've been thinking, I might do my dissertation on Duke Ellington.'

'You're studying History, aren't you?'

'It's all related. That's what I love so much about history.'

Her mum looked at her proudly and said: 'I think you're going to make your own history.'

'Whatever, Mum. You would say that!'

But her mum's prediction was about to come true – sooner than she thought.

In March 2015, Dina competed in the European Indoor Championships in Prague. As she flew over the city with John, she still had to pinch herself that athletics gave her the opportunity to visit such beautiful cities.

At the beginning of that year, her 60-metre time was hovering around 7.33. She'd worked on getting it down to 7.14 throughout February but wanted to improve on her personal best further.

'I want to get to 7.10, John.'

He told her: 'Go for 7.08 and you'll match Jeanette Kwakye's record.'

Jeanette was a three-time British champion who'd retired in 2014, and Dina made it her goal to equal her time.

In the heats she performed brilliantly and came in first at 7.10 seconds. She knew the final would be tougher, though; she would face Dafne Schippers, the fastest European woman.

John reminded her: 'Just concentrate on reaching your best.'

In the final, Dina spotted that Dafne was wearing her favourite purple and yellow Nike trainers. While Dina was in lane seven, Dafne was to her right in lane eight.

'I'm pleased I picked my pink ones,' Dina thought to herself. She took a final glance at her nails before she settled into the blocks. She'd decided on gold for this race, a bold statement for what she aimed to win.

'On your marks... get set...'

Bang!

Dina made a good start. With 20 metres to go she was leading, but it wasn't long before she felt the strength of the champion Dafne overtaking her to take gold. But as Dina crossed the finish line to take silver, she knew – even before checking the board – that she'd run a great time.

She hugged Dafne, who had run a record speed of 7.05 seconds, and then saw her own time flash up. It was 7.08. She had beaten her time and matched Kwakye's record. She ran over to the side to celebrate with John.

'I did it, John!'

Uncharacteristically for John, he was smiling away. 'Well done, Dina. Not only have you matched a British record, you're now the fastest teenager ever at 60 metres!'

Dina shook her head in disbelief. But, despite the record-breakers, she knew she couldn't relax yet. She had a full summer of athletics championships ahead of her: from the FBK Games in the Netherlands to the London Anniversary Games and the World Athletics Championships in Beijing. There were always more records to beat and champions to take on.

CHAPTER 18

HENGELO, LONDON, BEIJING, RIO

At the Fanny Blankers-Koen Games in the Dutch city of Hengelo, Dina was warming up in lane six, and chuckled to find herself next to Dafne Schippers once again. Not that this put her off: she looked down the track, feeling confident she was going to run a great 100 metres, and, if anything, she was thankful for runners like Dafne who spurred her on to be better.

She knew that Dafne was working towards running the race in under 11 seconds, which would set a new national record for her country. But Dina had her own goals. She'd worked solidly on the race with John and had reduced her time to 11.15 two weeks before in Manchester. Today, she wanted to break the British world record.

'On your marks, get set...'

Bang!

Dina blasted out of the blocks. It was an excellent start and for the first half of the race she was almost neck-and-neck with Dafne. But in the last 10 metres the Dutch champion took a clear lead and flew over the finishing line in a record breaking 10.94 seconds. Still, Dina had her own reason to celebrate too. She jumped for joy as her score flashed up on the board: 11.02 seconds. She'd smashed her own personal best but also broken the British world record for the 100 metres, beating the previous time of 11.05, held by Montell Douglas.

Dina arrived home to a hero's welcome at Blackheath and Bromley. They'd made her carrot cake: her favourite. The coaches and athletes gathered around, and they asked her what record she wanted to beat next.

Dina already knew. She had her heart set on running the 100 metres in under 11 seconds. If Dafne could do it, so could she.

* * *

Two months later, in July 2015, Dina took her chance at the London Anniversary Games. As she took in the clear blue skies surrounding the Olympic Park, she remembered three years earlier, when she stood at the side of the track as a box carrier, watching the athletes who would become the heroes of Super Saturday. She had hoped the races would attract crowds but never dreamt the stands would fill to their 40,000 capacity. She felt excited, rather than nervous. Although she wanted to achieve her next record, ultimately, she just loved to race. It was her first heat and she breathed a sigh of relief she wasn't racing against Dafne, although she knew Murielle Ahouré, to her left, was a strong contender with a speed of 10.81 seconds.

'On your marks, get set...'

Bang!

As Dina left the blocks, she told herself off. She'd not made a great start and Murielle led. But she lifted her knees high and pumped down the straight stretch to overtake and keep her at bay. When she crossed the line first she knew she'd run a good race. A roar went up from the crowd and she knew before she even looked at the board that she'd hit her record. There it was – yellow figures in stark contrast against the black background: 10.99 seconds. She put her thumbs up to the crowd and waved. She was the first British woman in history to run 100 metres in under 11 seconds.

As she joined her parents at the side, her mother could barely speak.

'I always feel kind of helpless when you run... but you amaze me every time!'

It was a fantastic achievement and Dina wanted to match or beat her new time in the final. But it wasn't to be. Dafne took gold, running an incredible time of 10.92, while Dina finished fourth with a time of 11.06 seconds. At the end of the race, they hugged each other.

Dina laughed. 'One day I'll catch up with you!'

'I think you will too. See you in Beijing, Dina!'

Their summer wasn't over yet. They were both competing in the World Championships in China that August.

* * *

In Beijing, Dina did not manage to qualify for the 100 metres final, but nevertheless watched in awe when Shelly-Ann Fraser-Pryce and Dafne Schippers took gold and silver respectively. She was also disappointed not to have the chance to visit any of the city's top tourist spots, but at least she had qualified for the final of the 200 metres, and the crowd at the Beijing National Stadium cheered as she and her fellow competitors prepared themselves for the race.

Dina had run two personal bests in the last two heats, even beating Dafne's times. However, as with every race, she knew it came down to her performance on the day. 'As long as I achieve another personal best,' thought Dina.

The gun fired and Dina took off down the track. She started well, but it was clear the race belonged to Dafne and the two Jamaicans, Elaine Thompson and Veronica Campbell Brown, who charged ahead to cross the finish line first. Dina came in at fifth place but she leapt up and down when she saw her time: 22.07!

Even though she hadn't won a medal, the spectators and press knew for sure now that the British athlete was incredibly special and had the potential to be a future world champion.

At 19 years old, she'd become the fastest teenager in history, a title previously owned by her hero, Olympic champion Allyson Felix. Her time of 22.07 seconds in the 200 metres also broke a British record set by Kathy Cook in 1984, 11 years before

Dina was born.

Dina's eyes shone as she spoke excitedly to the press: 'To run against such incredible elite athletes was an honour in itself. I've hit three PBs, three days running and am so happy to have ended with a record.'

* * *

A year later, Dina had to pinch herself to make sure she wasn't dreaming about competing in the 2016 Rio Olympics. She glanced up towards Corcovado, the mountain that overlooked the Olympic Stadium. Brazil had always appealed to her as an exciting and vibrant place with a fascinating history, with its melting pot of African and European cultures that had helped to create the offbeat syncopated rhythms of bossa nova.

Dina had come fifth in the 200 metres in an admirable time of 22.31. But it wasn't enough to beat athletes on the international stage. However, she had one last chance to win a medal in the relay team.

She was back with her old friend Desirèe Henry for the relay, along with new teammates Daryll Neita and Asha Philip. They'd spent the summer practising their performance on the new site at Loughborough and had built a great team dynamic. Asha, the eldest at 25, kept them in check when they lost their focus or when the impulsive nature of Daryll, the youngest, took hold. And their belief in their team grew stronger as they demonstrated their skill and strength at the European Championships, taking away silver, losing out to a strong Dutch team.

'On your marks, get set...'

Bang!

Dina watched as Tianna Bartoletta of the USA and Christania Williams of Jamaica shot off on the first leg. They'd both made the incredible starts everyone expected, but so had Asha and she wasn't far behind them before the first handover to Desirèe. Desirèe took the baton and covered considerable ground to take fourth place behind Jamaica, the USA and Germany, passing to Dina, who increased their lead on the third leg. After a seamless handover to Daryll, Dina cheered as she watched her ward off challenges on the home straight from Germany's Rebekka Haase to take third place behind the USA in first and Jamaica in second.

The British team leapt around for joy as the enormity of their win against the two athletic powerhouses sank in.

'Bronze! We've won a medal!'

They'd also broken the British record that night, with a new time of 41.77 seconds. As Dina stood on the podium with the rest of her team to claim bronze, she felt as though – from that moment on – anything was possible.

CHAPTER 19

A
SETBACK

It was the start of 2017 and Dina was performing plyometric jumps in one of her final training sessions before competing in the Birmingham Indoor Grand Prix. On the last jump, she misjudged the ledge of the bench and fell back on to the floor. She cried out in pain as she tried to get back up again. John rushed over and instructed her not to move. Dina winced as her physio, Martin Wilson, came over to take a closer look.

'No!' Dina cried out in frustration when she was told she had fractured her foot. She turned to John.

'Well, you definitely can't do Birmingham on Saturday.'

Dina's mind raced ahead to the World Athletics Championships that August. The games were being hosted in the Olympic Stadium in London and Dina was desperate to take part.

She was told her foot would take at least eight weeks to heal, and that it might not be possible to get back in shape in time for August.

Dina groaned. 'I can't believe it John – how stupid!'

'I know, don't kick yourself for it, though.'

Dina couldn't help but smile at his terrible joke, although the timing seemed incredibly unfair and inconvenient. But she wasn't going to let this jeopardise her career. Later that day she tweeted: 'So upset and frustrated but it was a freak accident, one of those unavoidable things in life, I guess. Comeback starts now.'

Dina held on to her dream to be part of the World Athletics Championships. There was no way she was going to miss that, not after experiencing the thrill of 2012 in the Olympic Stadium.

A few days before her operation she went to meet John and the Olympic relay team at a training session. As she arrived on crutches, the other girls in the relay team ran over to greet her.

'Oh Dina, it's so good to see you! But shouldn't you be resting?'

Dina looked at them defiantly. 'Guys, I'm going to make the team. We're a great relay team, do you think I'd let you down?! I want us to get silver this time – it's too important!'

They all avoided her eye contact as she continued to beam confidently at them. John also looked away.

'Just wait and see! I'm going to be able to run in August. So I might as well come to all the meetings. I don't want to miss out on team bonding.'

Desirèe looked at her with surprise. 'Dina, I can't believe how upbeat you are!'

Daryll shook her head. 'You're an inspiration.'

She shrugged. 'Oh guys, whatever.'

Dina put the doubtful faces of John, Martin and the relay team out of her mind as she underwent surgery on her foot to insert two screws. She'd heard stories of athletes who weren't able to run for two years after fractures, but she was determined that wouldn't be her.

Even so, it wasn't easy. The day after her plaster was removed, she gasped as she tried to put the kettle on to make a cup of tea. She couldn't even get on her tiptoes. She cried out in frustration. If simple tasks were this challenging, how would she rebuild the strength in her muscles for the Championships? She'd expected some muscle loss but was downhearted to discover just how much. It was April and she only had four months to be fighting fit for the Championships. It would be another three months until she could train properly too.

To add to her pressures, she was in her last year of university and needed to finish her dissertation. She vowed that she wouldn't waste a single hour of her time. In between poring over her academic notes and writing her dissertation at her laptop, she continued to focus on building up her muscle strength with John and Martin. As well as supervising her gentle exercises on an underwater treadmill, they worked on her balance and coordination too. By the first of July, Dina was preparing to run in the 100 metres in the British Athletics Championships in Birmingham. Her muscles weren't yet back to their full strength, but she felt strong enough to compete.

John looked at her in astonishment as she jumped up and down excitedly.

'It feels so great to be on spikes again!' she said.

And she had another reason to celebrate.

'I've finally got my dissertation in – yippee!'

'Please, Dina, save your excitement for the track.' John was hesitant to share in the celebrations, but he, like everyone else, was impressed with her positive mental attitude.

That day she came sixth in the 100 metres, achieving a time of 11.53 seconds. It was a slower time than any of her personal bests the year before. But it felt great to race again and she knew she was on the road to recovery and would continue to improve.

But there was one question hanging over her. Would she be fast enough to compete in the 200 metres or relay race at the World Championships in the Olympic Stadium? With just six weeks to go, there was little time to train for the event.

CHAPTER 20

WORLD CHAMPIONSHIPS: OLYMPIC PARK 2017

The roar from the crowd reverberated in Dina's ears as she shot out of the blocks and started to round the bend on the 200-metre track for the IAFF (now World Athletics) Championships at the Olympic Park. Their cheers of support, love and encouragement were all that she needed to power her down the home straight. Any doubts or fears she'd been feeling before the race melted away, and she soared towards the finishing line to take fourth place.

She looked up at the clock and grinned from ear to ear. She hadn't taken a medal, but she didn't care. She'd achieved a new personal best of 22.22 seconds, in front of one of the most supportive home crowds she'd ever experienced.

Dina hugged and congratulated the other competitors, and felt relieved that she'd trusted her own instincts and not listened to the doubts of people around her. She was on the road to recovery and felt ready to put the injury behind her. John shook his head in disbelief at Dina's flushed and happy face.

'I wouldn't have believed it was possible, Dina,' he said, 'after only six weeks of training.'

'John, that was amazing! I felt like the crowd was literally pushing me to the finish line!'

'They were right behind you, Dina.'

'Never doubt me again, eh, John?'

'I never did.'

'It might sound a little crazy, but I think this has done me good in the long term.'

John raised his eyebrows.

'Seriously, look,' she went on, 'a medal would have been fantastic of course. But I know what I'm capable of overcoming now. I'll face any other setbacks with more confidence.'

John smiled and, with a twinkle in his eye, said: 'Great! How about I break the other foot then?!'

Dina cried out in protest. 'John, that's not funny!'

A few days later, Dina was gearing up to perform in front of another packed London stadium. This time the crowd were cheering on Dina, Asha, Daryl and Desirèe as they prepared to run the 4 x 100 metres relay. They needed all the support they could get as they were about to take on the reigning champions: the USA and Jamaica.

Yet again, relief washed over Dina.

'I wouldn't have missed this for anything,' she thought as she made her way to the third leg on lane five and placed her marker on the track for the baton handover.

Relays were as problematic as any other race and the team knew they could never quite predict the outcome. They were facing a strong USA team that consisted of Allyson Felix and Tori Bowie. But when Dina looked down at her pink and yellow Nikes she felt confident. She had also applied eyeliner and eye shadow before the race, to help her relax. As she always said: 'If we win a medal, I want to be looking my best!'

Desirèe laughed. 'Won't it be smeared all over your face by then?'

'Extra waterproof, of course! In case I start crying!'

'On your marks... get set...'

Bang!

The USA and Jamaica proved to be tough competition and took the lead comfortably, just as the British team had expected. While Desirèe was pelting down the track on the second leg, Dina began to run in preparation for the handover. When she took the baton, Jamaica's Simone Facey and the USA's Morolake Akinosun had a clear 10-metre lead on her.

'I can make a difference here,' thought Dina as she fought her way down the third leg, hot on their heels. After she handed the baton to Daryll for the home stretch, she cheered her on. Daryll charged ahead of Jamaica's Sashalee Forbes to lead the team to a silver medal in a record time of 42.12 seconds.

Journalists gathered to interview a British team who understood the significance of what they'd achieved. To take a step up from bronze in Rio was fantastic enough but to do it on home turf meant the world to them. The team were so proud to win the medal in London.

But the celebrations weren't over for Dina that summer. The following week, she graduated from university with a 2:1.

'No more essays!' She danced around her room, thinking of the 61 essays she'd completed over the past three years. However, she wasn't sure she wanted to give up academia completely and began to consider studying law.

Her mum looked at her in astonishment.

'Dina, how about you give yourself a break for a little while?'

Dina joked: 'You know what would happen if I took too long a break, Mum, I'd just end up eating pizzas my whole life!'

But she knew her mum had a point. She was pleased to put the stress of studying behind her and focus on being a full-time professional athlete. For the next few months, she focused on training for her first ever Commonwealth Games in Australia.

The Games weren't until April 2018, but Dina flew out a month early to the preparation camp in Brisbane, an hour away from the Gold Coast venue. She wanted to get accustomed to training and competing in 28-degree heat. In a year without the Olympics or World Championships to compete in, she wanted to focus on the 200 metres at the Games and run against the fastest in the world. And, of course, it was great to train in warm temperatures in the early months of the year on the beach.

This time she was representing England, rather

than Team GB, and so, instead of a Union Jack, her kit was emblazoned with a single red lion.

A huge cheer went up from the crowd as the announcer read out the competitors in the 200 metres final: 'In lane six, Dina Asher-Smith!' It always made a difference to hear that support. Dina listened for the sound of her mum cheering, which always spurred her on in each race: 'Go on, Dina!' She was overjoyed her parents had flown across the world to see her compete and that her friends back home were organising sleepovers to ensure they stayed up and didn't miss her race.

To her right in lane seven was Jamaica's Olympic double gold medallist, Elaine Thompson, one of the fastest women in the world.

Dina told herself: 'This is why you chose to be here. To run and compete against the best. But forget all that right now. Just spring out of the blocks – and run!'

'On your marks... get set...'

Bang!

Dina flew out of the blocks and took a clear lead. But on the last 20 metres there was a challenge to her left as the Bahamian athlete Shaunae Miller-Uibo and Jamaican Shericka Jackson overtook her to take gold and silver respectively. But Dina had come in at 22.29 seconds to take bronze, just ahead of Elaine Thompson who'd taken fourth place, and so was ecstatic with her result.

But it wasn't the only medal Dina took away from the Games. Two days later she helped the women's Team England relay team take gold in a new British record of 42.46 seconds that defeated the defending Jamaicans.

She told John her goals for the coming year. 'I'm going to get my 200 metres in under 22 seconds. And I know I've got a 10.80 in me for the 100 metres.'

As she flew over Australia clutching her two medals, she thought ahead to the European Championships in Berlin that summer. She knew she had to work hard to keep her promise to John.

CHAPTER 21

EUROPEAN CHAMPIONSHIPS: BERLIN

In the call-up room, waiting to go out on to the track at Berlin's Olympiastadion, Dina could feel her nerves rising. She was about to run the final of the 100 metres. But even her usual distraction tricks of focusing on 'normal' things like hair and make-up weren't working. She'd been working hard all year to this point and she was happy with how she'd performed in the semi-final earlier that day, coming first with 10.93 seconds. She'd broken a record in Oslo in June of 10.92, beating her previous record of 10.99. But still, she felt uneasy.

Would she stumble? Would there be a headwind? There were fears she couldn't quite shake, for some reason.

John knew better than to distract Dina from her pre-race rituals, but he could see something was on her mind and that these were no ordinary race nerves.

'What's up, Dina?'

She sighed. 'I dunno.'

'Are you thinking about the start in your semi-final earlier?'

Dina nodded, with some relief. It was rare she could ever hide what she was thinking from John.

'It wasn't a bad start,' John said.

'No, it wasn't.'

'You know what, Dina, just do your normal start.'

'Normal?'

'Yes, normal.'

As she settled into the starting blocks, she realised they were the only words she had needed to hear. Two lanes to her left was Dafne Schippers, who she'd still never beaten.

'Normal start, Dina, normal start,' she repeated to herself.

'On your marks... get set...'

Bang!

She tore out of the blocks and took the lead from the start, a clear half-metre ahead of her competitors. She crossed the line first and leapt for joy as her time flashed up: 10.85 seconds!

'Yes!'

Dafne was one of the first to congratulate her. 'You got me, Dina!'

'I said I would one day!'

The next day Dina won gold in the 200 metres in 21.89 seconds, beating Dafne into second place.

It was a new record. Dina was now the fastest British woman in history and the first to run below 22 seconds for 200 metres.

But she continued to fly that week. In the 4 x 100 relay race, she was picked for the anchor leg, tearing down the home straight to beat off a challenge from the Dutch sprinter, Naomi Sedney, and take gold for Britain.

Dina took away three gold medals from Berlin. All eyes were on this star athlete, who was already demonstrating great Olympic potential for Tokyo.

John kept her grounded though. 'She's done okay,' he responded gruffly as the media clamoured to speak to her.

Dina shook her head. 'One day John, I'll make you cry.'

'Make that your next goal!'

'I will, John.'

Later that year, Dina was named Women's European Athlete of the Year and was hailed by Sebastian Coe as the next sprint sensation in athletics to follow in Jessica Ennis's footsteps. Not only had she become hugely successful during 2018, but also rather famous.

CHAPTER 22

WORLD CHAMPIONSHIPS: DOHA

Dina continued to train for the rest of 2018, but her success in Berlin and her newfound fame brought with it many exciting new opportunities. Towards the end of the year she was included on Forbes' 30 Under 30 lists, and asked to model for Paris Fashion Week.

John rolled his eyes and quipped: 'Well, this is all we need, you already spend enough time on make-up before a race!'

'The track is my red carpet, thanks John!

'Well, please, no shimmying down the track – we won't improve your times that way!'

Dina fell about laughing but was genuinely happy to be asked. She loved fashion and particularly enjoyed supporting British fashion designers. But in early 2019 she received the ultimate accolade when Stormzy asked her to be part of a collective of young and inspirational black Britons for a cover he was curating for the magazine *Elle*. Although she continued to shrug off suggestions that she was a role model, she was beginning to realise she had a voice to champion the causes she cared about. She began contributing to a women's sports column to celebrate women's achievements in sport and help tackle their under-representation in the media.

Despite her newfound fame, Dina knew she had to keep setting goals with John, in order to stay grounded and to avoid becoming complacent.

One morning, John called her up, just a week after she'd come back from a sport-launching event organised by Nike in Paris. She was still reeling from the fact that she'd met Naomi Campbell.

'Right, I know you've been swanning about with

celebs but if you're not down at Norman Park within the hour, I'm coming round there to drag you out.'

'John, I've just ordered a Domino's!'

'What? You do want to get below 10.85 seconds this year, don't you?'

'Okay, John, okay!' She groaned but was grateful for his grounding influence. No matter where she might go or whoever she might meet, she still had their training schedule to stick to for the new year: four hours a day, six days a week. She smiled to herself as she realised she couldn't ever see herself being coached by anyone else but John. The fact she'd stuck with him since she was nine said as much.

Throughout the summer of 2019, Dina ran some formidable times at the British Championships and Anniversary Games, but she hadn't yet matched her time of 10.85 for the 100 metres. She knew she would have to break her own record to beat Shelly-Ann Fraser-Pryce, who she lost out to on silver. And she was yet to run the 200 metres in under 22 seconds, a time that John was certain she could achieve.

However, the year still wasn't over. Expectations were running high for the World Championships in Doha that autumn and Dina put anything that might distract her or pile on the pressure to one side, which included a ban on social media four weeks up to the event. Bets were already on that she could be the first Briton to become a 200 metres gold champion, a feat not yet achieved.

***

As a gentle breeze blew around the Khalifa International Stadium in Doha, she knew she had to put the expectations of the crowd to one side. Dina thanked her lucky stars again that the 100 metres final was at night to avoid the intense temperatures of the day. She'd already felt her energy flag a little after the last two days of heats. But now, she had to run, run, run as fast as she could possibly could.

No matter that the world champion and sprinting legend Shelly-Ann was right next to her in lane six, with her multi-coloured hair sway from side to side in a ponytail. Shelly-Ann Fraser-Pryce – her hero, and now her equal.

Dina still had to pinch herself. She was running against such world-class athletes. 'Don't think about that now,' Dina told herself. 'The next 10 seconds are all that counts.'

'On your marks... get set...'

Bang!

As she took off down the track, she ran with all the passion and desire to win that she'd always had. But it wasn't to be, and she was beaten into second place and a silver medal by Shelly-Ann by 0.12 seconds.

But, at 10.83 seconds, Dina had still beaten her personal best and had set a new national British record. She was also the first British woman in 36 years to win a World Championships sprint medal.

During the medal ceremony, Dina was shocked

when Shelly-Ann looked down from the top podium and said to her: 'You're an inspiration. You'll be at the top soon. I'm sure of it.'

Dina felt the tears well up in her eyes as the enormity of those words began to sink in. With just one year to go until the Tokyo Olympics, she was moving closer to her dream.

But she still couldn't afford to get distracted. She had heats for the 200 metres the next day to focus on. Could she finally run it under 22 seconds? And win gold for her country?

Three nights later, Dina looked out on to the track of Khalifa International Stadium.

'This is it,' she said to herself. 'This is your race.'

She'd come top of the heats over the past two days, running 22.32 and 22.16 seconds, respectively. She was tired but knew she had reserved just enough energy for this last push, to run under 22 seconds for the final. Dina turned back to John and gave him a huge smile.

She could tell he was nervous. More than he

normally was. She knew how much this race meant to him, as well as her. But, as ever, he remained calm, repeating the words that had become customary before each race.

'Don't hold the horses, Dina.'

She nodded at him and smiled.

Yes, John believed in her but ultimately it was always down to her to deliver. And they both knew anything could happen in a race: a false start, a sudden headwind, a sudden burst of speed from a competitor. But as she walked on to the track and waved to the crowds, she felt an almost overwhelming sense of excitement build up inside her. She couldn't wait to unleash her excited energy on the track.

'On your marks...'

The crowd fell silent.

'Get set...'

Dina took one last look at her nails she'd painted a pale pink for the event.

She told herself: 'Just run – as fast as you can.' It

was the only thing she needed to tell herself in that moment.

Bang!

Dina flew out of the blocks. Above the roar of the crowd she tuned in for the cries of her mother that always helped to keep her centred in the race, while everything else passed by in such a flash.

Dina blazed around the turn, warding off challenges from the USA's Brittany Brown and Anglerne Annelus. As she went into the home straight she knew she had it. The race was hers. She crossed the line in 21.88 to take gold. She clasped her hands to her face as everyone ran to congratulate her. By running the race in under 22 seconds, she'd not only beaten her own personal best but made history for her country. Dina was now the first British female athlete to ever win a global sprint title.

She managed to contain her emotions until she saw the sight of her mum bounding down the steps of the stadium, with her dad following close behind, as always. Then the tears of relief and joy flowed. As she hugged them for what felt like an eternity, she felt a tap on her shoulder.

She turned to see John standing behind her and saw that his eyes were looking mistier than normal.

'Ha! Is that a tear in your eye, John?'

'You've done it. You've run the race I always knew you could run.'

Three days later, Dina brought home another medal for Britain, winning silver with Asha, Ashleigh and Daryll in the 4 x 100 relay, in 41.85 seconds. She returned home, a world champion and hero.

CHAPTER 23

THE FUTURE
IS BRIGHT

'It's funny, you may be a world champion but you look exactly the same!'

Mrs Carty stretched out her arms to greet Dina at the reception of Perry Hall Primary School.

Dina laughed. 'Hopefully I've grown a bit!'

'It's the smile, I think. It just hasn't changed.'

'Well, it has changed here,' said Dina as she walked the corridors of her old school.

'Wait till you see the track and field facilities, they've changed quite a bit.'

Dina was introduced to another teacher, whose face she recognised.

'My name's Louise,' said the teacher. 'I was the

year above you here.'

Dina replied, 'Oh yes! I remember you.'

'I look after the running club now. It's become so popular! All the kids want to do is join now they know you went here; you're a hero to them!'

Dina blushed. 'That's so great more kids want to get into athletics.'

She thought of the speech Darren had given at her secondary school. 'Whether or not they want to turn professional, there's nothing quite like just running in a straight line, the wind in your hair.'

She looked out of the window towards the field where she'd first raced Mrs Carty. How long ago it all was.

'Well, you've made it all look possible, you see.'

They made their way towards Dina's old classroom.

'They're very excited about seeing you,' said Louise.

'That's an understatement,' said Mrs Carty.

Dina heard the hushed whispers of: 'She's here!

She's here!'

Louise opened the door, and Dina saw a sea of excited faces staring up at her. Gosh, she thought, this is more nerve-wracking than running!

'Hello everybody!'

'Now, we're very lucky to have Dina with us today,' said Mrs Carty. 'As you know, she used to go to school here.'

Dina nodded. 'Yes, this place is very important to me as it's where I first started running.'

'Now, who's got a question for Dina?'

A slew of hands went up.

'Wow!' said Dina, who suddenly felt very overwhelmed.

'Please! Can we see your medals, Miss?'

'Yes, of course!'

The children all scrambled to take a close look as she took them off from around her neck.

One girl pointed at the gold medal she'd won in Doha. 'Is that from the Olympics, Miss?'

'Ah no, I've not won a medal for an individual

race in the Olympics. Well, not yet, that is!'

Another voice piped up: 'Are you going to win in Tokyo, Miss?'

Dina smiled. 'Funny, you're not the only one who's been asking me that, you know.'

Then she thought for a moment, and added, 'I will do all I can to win at Tokyo, yes.'

'Can you come back when you win the Olympics?'

Dina burst out laughing. 'I certainly will. And I'll make sure I'm wearing a laurel wreath on my head too.'

Olympic Medals

🏆 Rio 2016: 4 x 100 m Relay, Bronze

World Championship Medals

🏆 Moscow 2013: 4 x 100 m Relay, Bronze

🏆 London 2017: 4 x 100 m Relay, Silver

🏆 Doha 2019: 100 m, Silver;

4 x 100 m Relay, Silver;

200 m, Gold

NAME:	Dina Asher-Smith
DATE OF BIRTH:	4 December 1995
PLACE OF BIRTH:	Orpington, UK
NATIONALITY:	British
SPORT:	Athletics
Height:	164 cm
Main events:	100 m, 200 m & 4 x 100 m Relay
Club:	Blackheath & Bromley
Coach:	John Blackie

Olympic Medals

GOLD 0   SILVER  0   BRONZE 1

World Championship Medals

GOLD 1   SILVER  3   BRONZE 1

KATARINA JOHNSON-THOMPSON

For Nina

TABLE OF CONTENTS

PROLOGUE

It was a sunny April day on Australia's Gold Coast. Here, down under, it was autumn, but on the track at the Carrara Stadium, the athletes were wiping the sweat from their brows. It was as hot as a British summer's day.

Katarina Johnson-Thompson looked around the stadium, squinting to shield her eyes from the blazing sun. The stands were packed, including a generous number of bright yellow tops: Australian supporters wearing their national colour. Her fellow heptathletes came from eight Commonwealth nations, among them Canada, India, Belize, Ghana

– and of course, Australia. And because it was the Commonwealth Games, Kat, competing for England, would be running, jumping and throwing against athletes from Scotland and Northern Ireland.

Kat turned her focus back to the track and the long row of hurdles stretching out in front of her. The 100-metres hurdles was the first event of the seven that made up the heptathlon. Nerves fluttered in Kat's stomach. The hurdles were never her favourite event. The pressure always felt greatest at the start of the competition, and today she felt it more strongly than ever.

Although Kat was the reigning world indoor champion, she had never won an international competition outdoors – not since junior level. Over the last few years, she had experienced setback after setback, including battles with injury and self-confidence. Here on the Gold Coast, she had everything to prove.

But as she stood on the track in the bright

Australian sunshine, Kat felt a glow of positivity. Determination sparkled in her eyes. It was time to turn things around. She was ready!

The arena fell silent as Kat and her fellow athletes stepped into their blocks. But as the starting gun fired, the crowd erupted into noisy cheers of support. Kat made a strong start, springing nimbly over the first hurdles. But she had competition. On one side of her, Angela Whyte from Canada stormed into first place; on the other, Australian Celeste Mucci and the Canadian Nina Schultz moved into second and third.

Kat urged herself forward. She was pulling level with Nina in third. *Faster! Come on!*

But pressure from Kat sent the Canadian powering over the final few hurdles. Kat couldn't catch her. To the delight of the home crowd, Celeste, the Australian, finished first.

With six more events to go, Kat had plenty more opportunities to pick up points! Next was the high jump, her strongest discipline.

The English fans whooped as Kat flew elegantly over the crossbar, landing a stunning jump of 1.87 metres, taking her into first place.

The shot put was next. By now, night had fallen over the stadium, and blazing floodlights added to the sense of drama. Kat's heart was pounding as she stood in the throwing circle. This event was her weak point.

Kat frowned: 11.54 metres. It was over two metres short of the winning throw. From first position, Kat had slipped into third.

But the evening wasn't over. The final event of the day, the 200 metres, was one of Kat's strongest. It was time to deliver a rocket-propelled sprint!

And that's exactly what Kat did. Accompanied by enthusiastic whoops and cheers from the crowd, Kat powered straight into the lead. The other racers pounded the track, straining to catch her, but Kat was flying. *Over the line! Back in first place!*

Kat felt a glow of satisfaction as the day ended.

She knew to take nothing for granted in the heptathlon – with three events still to go, anything could happen. But for now, as the stars glittered high above the Carrara Stadium, Kat was in the lead. Gold-medal position!

Day two of the heptathlon dawned grey and overcast, but the enthusiasm of the crowd was as warm and noisy as ever. Kat felt a surge of excitement as she launched into her fifth event, the long jump. This was another of her best disciplines. She allowed herself a flicker of a smile as she clocked her distance: 6.50 metres. A strong jump. She had increased her overall lead.

And she was *still* in the lead after the javelin round.

As the runners lined up for the final event, the 800 metres, she gave a broad grin for the TV cameras. It was time to relax and enjoy herself!

As the starting gun fired, Angela Whyte strode into first place. Niamh Emerson, Kat's England teammate, darted into a strong second, followed by

Nina Schultz in third.

Kat trailed them in fourth. With two laps of the track to run, there was plenty of time to push forward. But when the moment came to make her move, her legs wouldn't let her. There was sharp pain in her right calf that grew with every stride.

Keep up, Kat told herself. *Keep up. That's enough.*

A painful two minutes later, Kat stumbled across the line in fourth. Her teammate, Niamh, had crossed the line in first. But a glance at the leaderboard sent Kat's heart soaring. She hadn't won the race, but victory was still hers! With a score more than 100 points higher than her closest rival, Nina Schultz, she, Katarina Johnson-Thompson, was the Commonwealth gold medallist!

As the gold medal was looped around her neck, Kat's pain was forgotten. Pride and jubilation flowed through her. This was her moment. Her first international gold!

And as the National Anthem played, Kat's mind flew ahead to the future. Following the

Commonwealth Games were the European Championships, then the World Championships, then the Tokyo Olympics. Standing here on the podium, it felt like the whole world was at her feet.

And Kat was determined to make a habit of winning!

CHAPTER 1

NASSAU

It was Tracey Johnson's first visit to the beautiful Caribbean island of New Providence in the Bahamas. She had come here as a dancer. Her troupe, the famous Bluebell Girls, performed all over the world: Paris, Rome, Madrid, New York, Toronto – and now Nassau, capital of the Bahamas. Every destination was special to the young dancers, and for Tracey, the trip to Nassau was to prove more special than most.

It was on Nassau's glittering beachfront, at the lavish Crystal Palace Hotel, that Tracey met her future husband, Ricardo Thompson. Tracey was performing there. Ricky was working at the hotel as a bellboy. There could be no more romantic setting to fall in love in, and that's exactly what Tracey did... with Ricky, and with this stunning Caribbean island.

Five years later, Tracey was still here in Nassau. She and Ricky had been together ever since that first magical meeting – and they were now expecting their first child. The couple decided to travel back to the UK for the birth. They reluctantly swapped the warm beaches and rustling palms of Nassau for the grey winter skies of Liverpool, home to Tracey's family. How cold it seemed to Ricky. How wet. How loud and bustling. Tracey too had got used to the sunshine of Nassau, the relaxed holiday vibe. Merseyside was going to take some getting used to!

On 9 January 1993, in the Liverpool suburb of Woolton, Katarina Mary Johnson-Thompson was born. Outside the rain was still falling, the sky was still grey. But as they bent over their newborn daughter, it was as if the Caribbean sun shone down on Tracey and Ricky. Around them, nurses and doctors smiled at the couple's delight.

'She's perfect!' said Ricky, rocking his tiny daughter in his arms.

'Little Katarina,' breathed Tracey. 'I wonder who she'll grow up to be.'

As the weeks and months went by, Ricky and Tracey watched as their little girl grew and grew. Every day brought new excitements. Smiles, gurgles, first words... Tracey and Ricky were enchanted, and they couldn't wait to take baby Katarina back to their island paradise.

First, though, they decided to get married. Friends and family gathered at the local registry office to listen as they exchanged their vows. Among the smiling faces was Katarina's, snuggled in the arms of her grandmother. Her happy squeals punctuated the ceremony.

'Do you have to go back to the Bahamas so soon?' asked her grandma.

'We miss it,' said Tracey. 'And we want little Kat to see it.'

It was true. Ricky and Tracey longed for their beautiful Caribbean home. Their plane tickets were booked, their bags packed, and one smiling baby was the final piece of very important luggage.

So, just a few months after Katarina's birth, the family was back in their small home in Nassau. Now it was the turn of Ricky's family and neighbours to meet little Kat. Wriggling and giggling in her pushchair, blinking her big brown eyes, Kat was adored by everyone. Even strangers on the street couldn't help grinning when they saw her.

'She's a blessing.'

'A very special baby.'

'A lucky baby.'

And of course, her parents agreed. Their beloved Kat was all of these things!

Tracey and Ricky soon settled into a happy routine. Ricky went back to his job at the Crystal Palace Hotel and rushed home after his shift to play with his little daughter, who was growing cleverer and more active every day.

But their bubble of contentment was about to be broken...

A year after returning from Liverpool to Nassau, Ricky came home from work with bad news.

'They're closing the hotel. Shutting it down completely. Tracey, I'm going to lose my job.'

Tracey stared at him in disbelief. 'They're shutting down the Crystal Palace? But – they can't! It's – it's—'

Tracey was lost for words. The huge Crystal Palace Hotel was the biggest landmark on the island. Its glittering towers, lit in rainbow colours at night, were the first thing visitors saw when they arrived by boat or plane. And of course, it was particularly special to her and Ricky. Without it, they would never have met.

Ricky hugged her. 'I'll look for work. It'll be okay.'

But as the weeks went on, it became clear that jobs were scarce. The hotel employed hundreds of staff members. It had been one of the biggest employers on the island. Some of the workers – waiters, porters, chefs, cleaners, receptionists – found jobs elsewhere, but many didn't, including Ricky.

'I wish I could help,' Tracey told him. But as a foreigner, it was almost impossible for her to find work.

Eventually the couple came to a painful decision. Tracey and baby Katarina would move back to the UK, where Tracey could find a job and support their daughter. Ricky would visit, and Tracey and Katarina would come back to the Bahamas whenever they could.

Ricky was heartbroken. 'But it's the only way to give her a future,' he said, cuddling Katarina tightly. 'The only way.'

So, with a heavy heart, Tracey packed her suitcases once again. This time it was for good.

CHAPTER 2

TOMBOY
IN A TUTU

Tracey and her daughter settled in Woolton, the Liverpool suburb where Katarina had been born, moving into the house shared by Tracey's mother, father and aunt. How different it was from Nassau, with its brightly coloured houses, sandy beach cafés and luminous turquoise sea. Swaying palms were replaced by ancient oaks and beech trees, and the bright sunshine by the changeable British weather: sun, showers, wind, hail...

From Woolton, with its big, comfortable houses, and its leafy parks and shops, it was a short bus ride to the centre of Liverpool. Here Tracey strolled around the iconic Albert Dock, with baby Kat in her pushchair. Everywhere she went there were reminders of the two things for which Liverpool was most famous: the Beatles, and Liverpool Football Club, or 'the Reds', who played at the city stadium, Anfield.

Tracey found work. She enrolled the lively Kat in nursery, and found a local ballet class for her as soon as she could toddle. Tracey missed her life as a dancer – the glitz and glamour, the thrill of being onstage... But she hoped Katarina might fall in love with ballet too. Tracey was determined to give her daughter the opportunity to follow in her footsteps, to discover this wonderful world of dance for herself.

Little Katarina was keen to please her mum. She went off to ballet class with a smile on her face, clutching a dance bag with her pink ballet shoes inside. She let Tracey dress her in a tutu and brush her dark curly hair into a neat little bun. Her mum came to watch the class sometimes, and Kat made sure to remember all the steps and smile while she did them. She knew how much her mum loved to watch her.

As the years went on, there were shows and ballet exams too. The walls of Kat's bedroom filled up with certificates, while her wardrobe filled up with leotards, tights and tutus. Her weekly schedule filled up with classes – ballet and tap. Kat was strong and graceful. All her teachers encouraged her, and Tracey started to get excited: her daughter had the makings of a professional dancer. Tracey's dream? That Kat would get a place at the Royal Ballet School. How proud she would be!

But Kat had a secret. She didn't really enjoy this world of pink and satin and spinning around to tinkling piano music. She would much rather be outside playing football! Her grandfather had introduced her to Anfield and Liverpool FC at a young age. Wearing her Liverpool shirt – Steven Gerrard, Number 8 – Katarina played as often as she could in the street near her house.

At school, St Mark's Primary in Woolton, sport

was quickly becoming Kat's favourite subject. She was one of the fastest runners in her class. Her teachers praised her sportsmanship and her determination. Kat was shy and quiet, but she had a strong competitive spirit.

'I'm going to win gold in the 100 metres this year,' she told her mum when the end-of-year Sports Day came round. 'Will you come and watch?'

'Of course.' Tracey hugged her. 'I wouldn't miss it for the world.'

Sports Day was Kat's favourite day of the whole year. She could hardly contain her excitement. As she sat impatiently through morning English and Maths lessons, her thoughts weren't on spellings or fractions. Her mind was already out on the field. She imagined the wind in her hair as she ran faster, faster, faster...

After lunch, it was finally time for the whole school to gather outside on the playing field. As usual, the teachers had organised all sorts of competitions: running, long jumping, relays – and even a sack race. Kat beat her classmates in almost everything. Crossing the finish line in first position and hearing Tracey's cheers of delight gave her a warm glow of pride!

Eventually it was time for the 100-metres final, the last race of the day. Only the fastest children were competing. As they waited on the start line, Kat felt a thrill of nerves and excitement. She grinned at Tracey who gave her an enthusiastic thumbs-up.

The Head of PE, Mr Willis, shouted, 'Ready, set, *go!*'

Kat and her schoolmates bounded away across the grass. The families shouted their encouragement. Kat reached maximum speed in just a few strides. Her feet were pounding the ground. Her arms were pumping. She couldn't go any faster. But wait – someone was catching her up. *No!* Kat eyed the finish line. Suddenly she found she could go faster. Her stride grew longer. Her arms pumped faster. She heard Tracey cheering. Without even noticing, she had crossed the line.

'Well done, Katarina! That was a brilliant run!' declared Mr Willis. He waited a moment while the runners got their breath back. 'Now, let's give out those medals!'

The kids who had come second and third stepped onto the podium. Shy Kat felt a flutter of nerves. Winning meant she would have to stand up there in front of everyone!

'And the gold medal goes to Katarina Johnson-Thompson!'

Eek! Here goes! Katarina stepped onto the podium and Mr Willis looped a shiny gold-coloured medal around her neck. There was loud applause from her schoolmates and their families. Kat beamed as Tracey took her picture. She loved the feeling of a medal hanging heavy around her neck!

And she couldn't wait for the chance to run again. She wanted to find out if she could push her legs even faster.

* * *

Kat was nine when she finally plucked up the courage to tell Tracey how she felt about ballet. She was quivering inside as she searched for the right words to use. She hated the idea of upsetting her mother.

'Mum, I–I–I don't think I want to do ballet anymore. I'm not enjoying it.' She paused, waiting for Tracey's reaction. 'Mum?'

Her mum stared back at her and Kat was worried she might cry.

At last Tracey spoke. 'But you've worked so hard, Kat. You've got so much promise as a dancer. Do you really want to give it all up?'

Kat nodded silently. She watched a tear rolled down her mum's cheek, and a guilty feeling clawed at her stomach.

But then her mum spoke again. 'It's okay, my love. I understand.' Tracey hugged her.

Kat felt like a heavy weight had lifted from her

shoulders. 'So does this mean I don't have to go to ballet class any more?'

'You don't have to do anything you don't want to do. I only wish you'd told me sooner, Kat.'

Kat beamed at her. 'You're not angry?' she asked.

'How could I be angry with you?' Tracey replied. 'You've tried your best. You've given your all.' Her daughter *always* gave her all. 'I'm so proud of everything you've achieved. I just want you to be happy, my love.'

So it was settled. No more ballet. No more leotards and tutus. No more dance exams. Her mum had just one condition: Kat needed another hobby to replace dancing.

Football?

Learning the keyboard?

Drama classes?

There were lots of options, and Kat tried them all. But nothing seemed to stick. It was running – running really, *really* fast – that made Kat happiest.

But running wasn't a hobby – was it?

CHAPTER 3

TAKING
A LEAP

'But I've never tried the high jump,' gulped ten-year-old Katarina. 'What if I can't do it?'

Mr Coakley, her teacher, smiled. 'You'll never find out if you don't give it a go, Kat. Here, we'll set the bar low to start with.'

The bar was a bamboo pole, taped to two metal stands. Below was a crash mat. A group of pupils, all wearing yellow St Mark's PE kits, had gathered around to watch.

Kat bent her knees and got ready to leap.

'You get a run-up,' said Mr Coakley, smiling.

Ah! Kat backed away from the pole to the other

side of the gym hall. She started to sprint towards the mat and the spindly bamboo pole, her long legs taking her higher with each step.

'Now, jump,' said her teacher.

Kat leapt into the air. She had expected to hear the crack of splintering bamboo as she crashed into the pole – but no! She sailed easily over it.

'Very good!' cried Mr Coakley. 'A round of applause for Kat's first high jump, please.'

Kat's classmates burst into loud applause. 'Go, Kat! Go, Kat!'

Kat beamed from ear to ear. 'Can I try a bit higher?'

Mr Coakley grinned. He'd known Kat's competitive spirit would quickly kick in. He raised the pole by a few centimetres. Once again, Kat bounded across the hall and cleared the pole with plenty of room to spare.

'Still too easy for you, eh, Kat?' he said. 'Let's give you a real challenge.' He raised the pole again. 'You can do it.'

Kat frowned. The pole looked really high this time. Surely she couldn't leap over that?

She shook out her legs. This time her run-up was slower, more calculated. She kept the pole in her sight with every step, and just as it seemed she was about to hit it, she leapt into the air, throwing every bit of energy into sending herself skyward.

She landed with a thump on the crash mat as her classmates let out a cheer.

'I did it?'

Mr Coakley's face was a mix of surprise and delight. 'You did it. You actually did it!'

Kat spun round. Yes, the pole had remained exactly where it was! She hadn't so much as touched it.

'Someone fetch a tape measure from the office,' Mr Coakley requested. 'Quickly. I think we might have a record here.'

Kat looked confused. A record?

Mr Coakley explained. 'The school high jump record has been in place for 29 years. It was set long before my time. But I have a feeling...'

A pupil came running back with the tape measure. Under the teacher's instruction, Kat and her classmates took the measurement.

'Just as I thought. Katarina Johnson-Thompson, you are officially a record holder! Twenty-nine years. My, my, this is quite an achievement.'

A grin lit up Katarina's face. She could hardly believe it. Until today she had never even tried the high jump! She couldn't wait to tell Tracey.

Mr Coakley looked thoughtful. 'I think you could have something special here, Kat. Now, off you go, kids, it's breaktime. Quietly now. I said – quietly!'

The children hurried out to the playground, sweeping Katarina up in an excited hubbub.

Mr Coakley shook his head in disbelief. 'That was extraordinary,' he said to himself. 'I can barely believe it. Imagine what she'd be able to do with some training.'

And an idea popped into his head.

The Harriers.

Later that afternoon, while Katarina recounted her record-breaking jump to Tracey back at home, Mr Coakley made a call to the Liverpool Harriers. Everyone in the city knew about the Harriers. They were one of the most famous athletics clubs in the country, founded 150 years ago. The Harriers team competed all over the country in all sorts of events: running, jumping, throwing, hurdles, cross country, marathon – the list went on and on. Their coaches were among the best in the UK and they were always on the lookout for talented young athletes to join their junior section.

Katarina was ten, old enough to join the junior section, and the Harriers arranged for a scout to come and watch her perform. Kat could barely contain her excitement. She felt a thrill that she had never felt before a ballet show. The Harriers! Training from professional coaches! She had never wanted anything so badly.

When the day came to perform for the scout,

Kat excelled. She pushed herself to run even faster than usual. She impressed the scout with her high jump and her long jump – and with her calm determination. Her strength of focus was clear to everyone watching.

'She's got potential,' the scout declared. Turning to Kat, he asked, 'Would you like to join the Harriers, Katarina?'

Kat could only nod. Her head was spinning. She knew she had done her best, but she had hardly dared hope they might want her.

Her teacher spoke for her. 'I think that's a yes!' he said.

At last, Kat found her voice. 'Yes! Yes, thank you!' she gasped. 'Oh, I'll train so hard. I won't let you down! Thank you!'

CHAPTER 4

THE HARRIERS

Athletics was just the hobby that Kat had been looking for. The Harriers junior section trained on Tuesday night and Kat fizzed with excitement every time she waited for the bus to take her from school to the grounds. In her bag was her yellow Harriers vest with its blue harrier logo, her most treasured possession.

Kat's coach was Val Rutter. Along with the Harriers' head coach, Mike Holmes, Val trained some of the Harriers' best athletes – some of them had gone on to perform on the UK athletics team. Young Katarina was a natural athlete, everyone could see that. Expectations were high – and training this talented newcomer would be a serious matter!

Kat's running was already strong. Under Val's instruction, she learnt the difference between sprinting and longer races. Val showed her how to spring out of the blocks and deliver a rocket-paced sprint. She taught Kat how to run longer races, conserving her energy so she didn't run out of puff halfway around the track. She was delighted to find out that Kat was good at both!

Next Val introduced Kat to hurdles. For several weeks, they did practice drills, learning techniques. Val showed her how to swing her legs over the hurdle one at time. Then Kat practised jumping over, leading with one leg then the other.

'My legs ache,' Kat grimaced. 'In weird places!'

Val smiled. 'Then you're doing something right. Hurdling uses a whole new set of muscles. I think you're ready to try the real thing now, Kat.'

Outside on the running track, Val had set up a line of hurdles, waist-high barriers planted at intervals of several metres all the way along the lane.

'This is a tough event,' she explained. 'Hurdles require speed, strength and flexibility, as well as coordination and balance. Think you can do it?'

Kat was always up for a challenge. Her legs were tingling and her mind was already whirring, calculating how to combine the sprint, the jump and the landing.

'I'll give it a go!' she grinned.

'The most important thing is not to hesitate in front of the hurdle. That's how people get hurt. Just go for it, Kat!'

Kat bounded fearlessly off the starting line towards the first hurdle. Safely over! The next hurdle loomed immediately. Over again! It was only when she got to the last hurdle that she stumbled. Her foot caught the top and she toppled to the ground. She rolled on to her back with a laugh.

'That was great for a first attempt, Kat,' said Val. 'Let's try again. And don't leap too high. That'll take away your momentum.'

This time Kat cleared all the hurdles cleanly. 'Is there anything you're not good at, Katarina?' laughed Val.

Kat scrunched up her face. 'Er... throwing?' Throwing had always been her weak point. At school there were lots of kids who were much better than she was.

'We'll work on it,' Val told her.

So they did. The next session began in the throwing circle. Kat and her junior teammates were going to learn the shot put.

First they passed the 'shot' around the group so everyone could feel the weight of it.

'It's so heavy! What if it lands on our feet?' one girl asked.

'Has anyone ever got hit?'

'Can we spin around before throwing it, like they do on TV?' said another.

Val looked stern. 'No hitting each other, please. And no spinning. That's called a "wind-up" and it's much, much harder.' She took the shot and raised it to her jaw. 'Right, step back and watch, everyone.'

With Kat and her friends at a safe distance, Val balanced herself at the edge of the circle. She made a sharp half-turn, and flung her arm out, sending the shot soaring through the air before it thudded down onto the grass.

'How did you make it go so far?' Kat asked in amazement.

Val explained. 'The trick is to use your whole body for momentum, not just your throwing arm.' She demonstrated again. 'See – my legs are bent and when I turn, my whole body is powering the shot. Let's do some drills. We'll start off without the shot.'

The group groaned. They hated drills. They wanted to start throwing straight away. But not Katarina. She loved to learn new techniques. For every event there were tricks to learn to make her performance the best it could possibly be. She listened attentively as Val told them how to hold the shot, how to stand, and the best way to shift their weight from one leg to the other.

But when they started to throw, Kat didn't find it easy. She visualised the shot flying long over the grass. In reality, it travelled just a few metres before falling back to the earth. Everyone else's shots were going further.

It was the same when they tried the javelin. Kat's legs gave her momentum, but her shoulders and arms weren't strong enough to give power to the throw. The frustration showed in her face.

'Early days, Kat,' Val told her.

But in the long jump and high jump, Kat shone. Mr Coakley's bamboo pole was a distant memory. Now Kat and her friends trained with a proper high jump: a pole supported by a stand, and a landing area as thick and bouncy as a trampoline. Kat was tall for her age, and her long legs helped her spring up and over the crossbar, landing impressive jumps. In the long jump, she bounded energetically along the run-up, sprang gracefully from the take-off board and kicked her legs in mid-air before landing in the sandpit. Each time she jumped further and her smile got broader. This was so much fun!

As the months went by, Val became more and more impressed with her protégée. Not only was Katarina talented, but of all the young athletes she trained, Kat was also the most dedicated. Even on the darkest, coldest winter evenings, when the other kids would start to drop away, preferring warm living rooms and the glow of their phone and TV screens, Kat would always be out there on the track, training under the floodlights with a smile on her face. She was determined to push herself as hard as she possibly could – and Val was determined to give her all the support she needed.

So too was Tracey. Kat's decision to swap tights and tutus for track and field had disappointed her mum – but she knew deep down that it was the right choice. She celebrated her daughter's achievements session by session with just as much enthusiasm as she had celebrated her ballet successes. Meanwhile, in the Bahamas, Ricky also followed Kat's progress, his face glowing with pride and pleasure as she told him all about her training on the phone.

Kat had found her passion, and supporting her from both sides of the globe, her parents could not be happier.

CHAPTER 5

TRACK TRIUMPH

In January 2005, Kat turned 12. She had moved from her small primary school, St Mark's, to nearby St Julie's Catholic High School, where she made a group of firm friends: Jodie, Olivia, Charlotte and Lauren. The girls all had their passions. Jodie, for instance, loved English and acting. She was in every one of their school plays and performances and wanted to be an actress.

Kat worked hard in all subjects, but sport remained her favourite. She was shy and modest, but all her friends knew her dream: to be a professional sportsperson.

The Harriers' sports ground in Wavertree, south Liverpool, had rapidly become Kat's second home. Her skills and strength were improving every week, and Val eventually knew she was ready to start competing.

The Harriers Under-13 Girls were part of the Youth Athletics Northern Premier League. Kat would be competing at the most iconic arenas in the north of England: the Gateshead International Stadium, the Don Valley in Sheffield... This was the moment Kat had been waiting for!

Her first year of competition brought a flurry of successes:

The Merseyside County Championships in Liverpool: first in the high jump.

Blackpool Open Medal Meeting: first in the 800 metres.

The Youth Athletics League Final in Birmingham: first in the 70-metres hurdles; third in the high jump.

Kat's bedroom was quickly filling up with medals.

But it wasn't just about winning. Kat was part

of a team now. She loved cheering on the other Harriers girls almost as much as she loved being out on the track herself. All the points that the girls won contributed to a team total, and the Under-13s were storming up the League. Indoors, outdoors, rain or shine, nothing could keep the smile from Kat's face.

But the world of competition brought new challenges. In athletics, anything could go wrong at any moment. A stumble in the hurdles. A sudden gust of wind. The flick of a ponytail knocking a wobbling crossbar off its stand. The road to success wasn't always smooth and Kat's confidence was easily dented by a mistake or a disappointing performance. She hated the feeling that she could have done better. And the more success she had, the more she struggled with self-doubt when she failed to come first.

But a sense of confidence and resilience came to Kat from a surprising source.

After athletics, Kat's biggest passion was for

Liverpool FC. Over the years, she had seen them rise to glory than fall dramatically back down the league table. It was a rollercoaster of emotions for their fans – including 12-year-old Kat.

On 25 May 2005, Kat was glued to the TV as Liverpool played in the UEFA Champions League Final against AC Milan at the Atatürk Olympic Stadium in Istanbul, Turkey. Milan were the favourites. If Liverpool didn't win, they would not qualify for the competition next year. All Kat's hopes were on the pitch with her beloved Reds.

There was instant disappointment. Within the first minute, Milan's captain, Paolo Maldini, scored. Kat howled with despair. Too soon!

Twelve nail-biting minutes later, Milan scored again. As the Milan fans cheered, the camera panned to the Liverpool crowd, their faces wide-eyed with dismay. Kat could hardly watch. Her team defended attack after attack. Surely they couldn't hold out much longer?

They didn't. Another Milan goal followed. The

first half ended 3–0.

That's that, Kat thought. *It's over.* Along with hundreds of millions of fans across the country, she was resigned to Liverpool losing.

But as the second half began, Liverpool's fortunes seemed to be turning. They missed two chances. Then Steven Gerrard scored with a header. 3–1! Kat's heart thudded in her chest – from dark despair, there was a glimmer of hope. The cheers of the Liverpool crowd were ear-splitting.

Minutes later there was another Liverpool goal, from Vladimir Šmicer. 3–2!

Then another, from Xabi Alonso. 3–3!

Was it possible? Could Liverpool actually win the match?

But Kat's joy was mixed with anxiety. There were still twenty minutes to go! She watched, barely able to breathe, as the ball flew from one side of the pitch to the other. Liverpool attacked. Milan defended. Milan attacked. Liverpool defended. At the final whistle the score remained 3–3.

The match would go to extra time.

Kat could see how tired the players were – but every one of them continued to give their all. Both Liverpool and Milan had chances, defended desperately by their goalies. The crowd were on their feet. The tension was extraordinary.

When the referee's whistle blew again, it was to signal a penalty shoot-out.

As the TV commentator reeled out penalty statistics, Kat's eyes were fixed on the Liverpool strikers, led by Steven Gerrard, the captain. Could they keep their focus? Would the Milan goalie make a mistake? Worse, would the Liverpool goalie make a mistake?

Milan took the first penalty. The ball hit the crossbar – and Kat squealed with delight.

Dietmar Hamann stepped up to take the next shot for Liverpool. The ball flew into the net! Kat cheered. 1–0!

Milan's next shot was heading straight for the back of the net – but the goalie dived low to save it.

Still 1–0.

Liverpool scored next. 2–0!

Milan scored. 2–1.

Liverpool's next penalty was saved by the Milan goalie. Oh no – was the tide turning again?

Milan scored with the next kick. 2–2.

Vladimír Šmicer was next to kick for Liverpool. The ball flew into the back of the net. Liverpool were 3–2 up.

Milan's Andriy Shevchenko stepped up. Kat gripped the edge of the sofa. If he missed, Liverpool would win. She stared at the TV, unblinking, watching as the ball shot towards the back of the net. The goalkeeper, Jerzy Dudek, hurled himself to the right – the wrong way! But suddenly Dudek's arm shot out to the left, stopping the ball. The penalty was saved. Liverpool had won!

Finally, Kat drew breath. Along with ten thousand fans in the stadium, and hundreds of millions worldwide, she let out an ecstatic cheer of joy and relief. No one had expected this. The Reds had won against all the odds. Even the manager, Rafael Benítez, looked shocked.

The match in Istanbul would stick in Kat's mind for ever. The memory would return to her whenever she felt herself falling behind, whenever her confidence was low. She had learned a valuable lesson.

Anything was possible. Never rule out the underdog!

CHAPTER 6

INDECISION

Under Val's dedicated coaching, Kat continued to shine in the high jump and long jump. Her skills in the other events were going from strength to strength too. She was training five days a week now, and her strength, stamina and skill were constantly improving.

But as Kat's collection of trophies and medals continued to grow, her friends and family had a question on their minds.

'Which event do you like best?' asked her friend Jodie. 'Do you know what you want to specialise in?'

Specialise? Kat frowned. She knew that most

athletes ended up focusing on one event. But it hadn't occurred to her that she too would have to choose between the sports she loved. She liked jumping, of course. High jump and long jump were where she got her biggest scores. But she also loved to challenge herself. Throwing? She was getting better at throwing at every session. She enjoyed the feeling of working hard and seeing the results each week.

'I–I don't know,' she stammered. 'I love all of them. I couldn't decide.'

Jodie grinned. 'Typical Kat! So indecisive!'

It was true. Kat was known for her indecision. Whether it was pizza toppings or what to wear to go out, Katarina always struggled to choose. Her friend didn't have that problem. Whereas Kat threw her energy into everything she did, Jodie was focused on drama, and drama alone – to the frustration of her other teachers!

'Maybe I won't have to decide.' Kat's face lit up. 'There's always the heptathlon. I could be a heptathlete.'

'Like Denise Lewis?'

'Exactly.'

Katarina loved to watch the heptathletes competing. She admired how versatile and skilled they were, like athletic superheroes! Of course, she enjoyed the drama and excitement of the big sprint races, the 100 and 200 metres. The sprinters were the megastars of the arena. But she followed the fortunes of the 'multi-eventers' with particular interest. The heptathlon, for the women, was all about endurance: seven events across two days. They started with the 100-metres hurdles, followed by the high jump, then the shot put and the 200 metres on day one. Day two was the long jump, the javelin, and finally the 800 metres. Meanwhile, the men competed in a 10-event version called the decathlon. In both cases, the points system was complicated. Kat watched with fascination as the athletes' scores accumulated between events. She got to know who was strongest in which discipline and where their weaknesses lay. She liked hard work – and no one in athletics worked harder than the heptathletes!

It turned out Val was thinking about the heptathlon too.

'It makes sense,' Val told Mike Holmes. 'Her high jump is outstanding, but she's so versatile too. She really is good at everything.'

Head coach Mike had been taking a keen interest in Kat's progress since she joined the team. He nodded. 'Let's train her for the heptathlon. I can't wait to see what she can do.'

So it was settled. It was time to combine Kat's skills. She would be a heptathlete and she couldn't wait!

In August 2006, 13-year-old Kat took part in her first multi-event competition: the pentathlon at the Amateur Athletic Association Under-15s Combined Events Championships. Pentathlons featured just five out of the seven events of the heptathlon: no javelin or 100 metres. At indoor events, the pentathlon always replaced the heptathlon – for a start, there simply wasn't room to throw a javelin indoors!

Kat finished sixth at the end of the competition, scoring a total of 2,748 points.

'Good job, Kat,' said Val with a smile.

From the sidelines, her mum had watched every step, jump and throw. 'I'm so proud of you, darling!' she said. 'That was amazing.'

Kat had earned her highest ever scores in long jump and high jump, competing against older girls. Running, jumping and throwing against the older teenagers hadn't phased her. She had loved the buzz of the stadium and the thrill of a tough competition.

'I had so much fun,' she beamed. 'I can't wait to try the full heptathlon!'

Kat's performance had given her an Under-15s pentathlon ranking of 15th in the country. She was ranked number 34 for the long jump and tenth for the high jump. Val and Mike knew this was just the start, though. Talented Kat had much, much more to give, they were sure of it.

They were right. The following year, 2007, Kat won gold at the Sainsbury's English Schools Championships; gold in the high jump at the England Athletics Under-15s Open Championships; gold in the high jump at the English Schools Combined Events pentathlon; gold in the England Athletics Under-15s Open Combined Events Championships pentathlon; gold at the England Athletics Under-15s Open Combined Events Indoor Championships pentathlon.

'This is getting silly,' laughed Jodie. 'No one needs that many medals! What ranking are you now, Kat?'

Kat shrugged modestly. 'Well, um, second in the Under-15s long jump. First in the high jump. And first in the pentathlon.'

'Seriously!' Jodie let out a squeal. 'Kat, that's incredible. Why do you keep this stuff to yourself? It's amazing!'

Kat blushed. 'They're just numbers, aren't they?'

'Just numbers?' squealed Jodie. 'Just numbers! You're one of the best young athletes in the country. In. The. Country.'

'Jodie Comer!' Kat ruffled her friend's hair. 'What about you? You danced for Craig Revel Horwood!'

It was true. Jodie and a group of girls from their school had won a national competition, Boogie For Your Bones, judged by the most brutal of the *Strictly Come Dancing* judges, Craig.

'But you don't see me making a secret of it, do you!' laughed Jodie. 'Unlike you, national champ!'

It was becoming harder to for Kat to keep her athletics success quiet though. In 2008, she won another string of gold medals, at the Under-17s Indoor Championships, the English Schools Championships, English Schools Combined Events and the England Athletics Open Championships. And while *she* didn't like to shout about her achievements, her teachers did. Shy, modest Kat hated assemblies where her name was read out and the whole school turned to stare at her. Being in the spotlight made her want to shrink into the floor – especially with Jodie and her other friends whooping noisily by her side!

CHAPTER 7

ITALIAN JOB

Warm Mediterranean sunshine was streaming down on a packed sports stadium in the small town of Bressanone, in northern Italy. Kat had never seen such a beautiful location for an arena. The track was fringed by lush fir trees. Beyond the trees were rolling green hills, with huge cloud-topped mountains in the distance. The sky was a luminous blue and the air was crystal pure. Kat breathed deeply and took in the scene with shining eyes.

The stands were packed with spectators, enjoying the sunshine and eagerly awaiting the first events. There were journalists too – for this was the World

Youth Championships, Kat's first international competition. All her competitions so far, all of her training and hard work had been leading to this moment, when she would compete alongside athletes from Europe, Africa, Asia, the USA, and even her dad's home country, the Bahamas.

The pressure was on. It was 2009 and the London Olympics, in 2012, were already on everyone's lips. Among these teenage sportspeople were future Olympians. Would 16-year-old Kat be one of them? To compete at the London Olympics was her goal, her dream...

First though, she needed to impress here in Italy.

So far, Kat's best combined score was 5,343. Her points tally had been rocketing upwards with every competition, but she knew she could still do better. Her secret hope? To achieve personal bests in all seven disciplines.

Day one began, as usual, with the 100-metres hurdles. Kat always felt nervous about the hurdles. There was so much that could go wrong. If she tripped over just one hurdle, the race would be over.

But she needn't have worried. As soon as the starting gun fired, she was away, sailing effortlessly over the hurdles. As she charged over the line, the cheers of the crowd rang in her ears. A personal best! What a way to start the competition!

Now that the hurdles were over, Kat felt more relaxed. She was enjoying herself in the bright summer sunshine. The high jump was next, bringing Kat another personal best.

The shot put and the 200 metres followed and Kat gave strong performances. The first day had gone by like a dream. Kat loved competing in front of this enthusiastic crowd. Even the presence of cameras and journalists couldn't put her off her stride.

Day two began with the long jump and Kat's biggest achievement so far. She jumped an epic 6.31 metres. It was a third personal best, and her biggest improvement yet!

Next was the javelin – another solid effort – and then the final event, the 800 metres.

Kat was top of the leader board. If she could beat the Latvian athlete Laura Ikauniece, her nearest challenger, in this last race, the gold medal was hers.

Mike Holmes was waiting on the touchline. The Harriers head coach had recently taken over her training. 'This is a good event for you, Kat,' he said. 'You're tired, I can see it. But you've still got it in you, if you want it enough.'

Kat's legs felt like lead. Her whole body ached. But she knew that the moment she stood on the start line, it would be a different matter. 'I can do this,' she replied, smiling.

As the starting gun fired, Kat felt a familiar energy surging through her body. Adrenaline. Her brain urged her long legs forward, and her legs obeyed, powering up to a stride. Running 800 metres would take her twice around the track. She must not lose sight of Laura.

Halfway round. *Keep ahead*, she told herself. *Keep ahead!*

One lap. *Keep up the pace!*

Two hundred metres to go. All the girls would have kept something back – that final bit of strength to allow them to sprint for the finish. Kat knew every single one of them would give it their all. She mustn't let anyone past. Especially Laura. *Pick up the pace! Go for it! Sprint! Sprint!*

The muscles in Kat's legs were screaming. Laura was beside her. She could feel her pumping arms and legs, churning the air. She was dimly aware of the shouts of the crowd. *Dig deep!* she thought. *Come on!*

Kat tumbled across the finish line and collapsed on to the track. She had kept Laura behind her. She had done it. She had won.

As she lay looking up at the bright blue sky, she realised: she, Katarina Johnson-Thompson from Liverpool, was World Youth Champion!

The other girls buzzed around her, offering hugs

and congratulations. Laura Ikauniece, who had won silver, and Kira Biesenbach, from Germany, the bronze medallist, set off around the track for a victory lap. But Kat was too exhausted to move. When she finally summoned the energy to use her aching legs, she had the track to herself. Someone handed her a Union Jack and she jogged slowly around the stadium, holding the flag high, smiling, as the crowd cheered her on. This was her moment. Every one of her hopes and dreams had been focused on winning an international competition.

It felt right. Shy, modest Kat was where she wanted to be.

Once the victory lap was over, Kat returned to the touchline, where Mike and her two biggest fans, her mum and grandmother, were waiting. They had been watching every step, leap and throw of the competition.

Her mum pulled her into a hug. 'I'm so proud of you, my love,' she whispered. 'You deserve this.'

Mike was grinning ear to ear. 'Great performance,

Katarina – 5,750 is a terrific score. And five personal bests! That long jump would have been enough to win an individual gold. You did yourself proud.'

But Kat's smile was wavering. 'I could have done better,' she said quietly. In her mind were the seven personal bests that she had wanted to achieve. It was always the throws – the shot put and javelin – that let her down and lowered her score.

Mike nodded. One of the things he liked most about Kat was her drive. She never stopped pushing herself. 'There's plenty of time, Kat,' he smiled. 'Don't let anything take away from what you've done today.'

And she didn't. Up on the podium, receiving her gold medal, Kat cried tears of pride and happiness. As the National Anthem rang out across the stadium, and the Union Jack was raised up the flagpole, it felt like a dream, completely surreal. *I made this happen*, she thought to herself. *This is the best day of my life. This is what I want to do. This is who I want to be.*

CHAPTER 8

A FAIRY GODMOTHER

The London 2012 Olympics were still three years away, but all eyes were already on the competition – including Kat's. Would she make the grade in time to compete alongside the likes of Jessica Ennis at the Games?

Mike was cautious. Kat was World Youth Champion. He knew she was more talented than even Jessica Ennis had been at sixteen. Kat had achieved the highest score at Under-18 level in the whole of British heptathlon history, beating Jess's record. But he had seen plenty of talented youngsters reach their peak in their teens then drop away. Could Kat sustain her potential? Did she have what it took to compete at senior level?

Deep down, Mike felt sure Kat had much more to give. It was his job to make sure she kept on growing as an athlete, and he was formulating a plan. There would be plenty of hard work to come: strength training, weights, more focus on Kat's weaker events – those troublesome throws. But it was important that Kat didn't crumble under the pressure. She was still a teenager. She had only just finished doing her GCSEs! Kat loved sport with a passion and Mike wanted to keep it that way.

There was a problem though...

The Harriers training ground in Wavertree was becoming too small to nurture a promising young athlete like Kat. The equipment needed updating. Everything was crammed together. Mike watched as Kat practised her high jump – she could barely take three strides before she leapt. *She needs a proper run-up*, he thought. *She needs to go to Sheffield or Manchester for training*. The high jump facilities there were much bigger and better equipped. *And she needs a gym membership.*

Mike sighed. All these things would require money. Kat had a Lottery grant that covered some of her training costs, but neither the Harriers nor Kat and her mum would be able to afford the extra expense. London 2012 would only happen for her if they could find help somehow.

If only a fairy godmother would wave her magic wand.

***

'There's post for you, Kat,' called Tracey. 'I don't recognise the handwriting though.'

Behind Tracey, in the kitchen, Kat was wrestling with her sports bags, which were overflowing with kit. Travelling light was not an option for a heptathlete with seven events to prepare for. Lugging her equipment on the bus between home, school and Wavertree was one of the things she liked least about training.

'Handwritten?' Kat spun round. Who would be writing her a letter? 'Do I have time to read it? I can't miss the bus.' She glanced at the kitchen clock. Just enough time.

She tore open the envelope. The header read 'Barrie Wells Sports Foundation'.

'Oh!' she cried as she started to read. 'Oh. Wow!'

'Who's it from?' asked Tracey, glancing over her shoulder. 'What does it say?'

'It's from someone called Barrie Wells. He is looking for young athletes to fund ahead of the Olympics. He's offering to fund me: £8,000 a year for training and equipment and whatever else I need.'

Tracey's eyes grew wide: £8,000? That was a huge amount of money.

'He funded Jessica Ennis. He paid for her physiotherapy. He's funding Steph Twell, the 1,500-metres runner, and Hannah Miley, and lots of others. He supports 18 young athletes every year.'

It seemed almost too good to be true!

Kat continued reading. 'His grandfather was a pole-vaulter and world record-holder, called, er... Ernest Latimer Stones. He says he loves sport and has chosen this way of using his wealth to help people. Mum, this is amazing. I'll be able to travel to Sheffield for training. And Manchester. I'll be able to get new equipment—'

'You'll be able to get a taxi to Wavertree so you don't have to carry all those bags about,' added her mum. 'It sounds like a brilliant opportunity, Kat.'

Mike was also delighted when he heard the news. 'Congratulations, Kat! Barrie is from Liverpool, you know,' he added. 'He's a huge football fan.'

Kat grinned. 'He must be okay, then!'

So it was agreed. Kat accepted Barrie's funding and in return, she became an ambassador for his sports foundation, which also provided access to sports for seriously ill children across the country. Everyone around Kat breathed a sigh of relief. It hadn't been a fairy godmother Kat had needed – it had been a fairy godfather!

And there was more...

Barrie knew how much Kat loved Liverpool FC. She had told him about playing football in the street as a child, wearing her Number 8 shirt, while her mum wanted her to be doing ballet practice. Barrie had organised a special surprise for her. Together they travelled to Anfield, where her showed her to his executive box overlooking the halfway line.

'You're a VIP today, Kat,' he told her as they climbed the steps. 'There's someone I'd like you to meet.'

As he flung open the door, Kat's eyes fell on the smiling face of Steven Gerrard. Number 8. Her Anfield hero! Kat's expression flicked from shock to amazement to elation. She was in the same room as Steven Gerrard!

'Consider it a reward for your amazing World

Youth Championship performance,' Barrie told her.

'I can't believe it!' laughed Kat. 'This is even more exciting than a medal.'

CHAPTER 9

OUT OF ACTION

Just ten days after her Italian triumph, Kat was on a plane to Serbia to compete in the European Under-20s Championships. With two major championships in under two weeks, she had to learn techniques for recovery. Her body had never worked so hard.

She triumphed again. This time as she stepped onto the podium, Kat was crowned European Junior Champion. Her score was 400 points higher than Jessica Ennis's had been at sixteen. Mike felt more and more confident in the sparkling young heptathlete.

But, back in Liverpool, there was a niggle of worry in Kat's mind.

Her left knee was giving her pain every time she jumped. Her left leg was the one she used for take-off. Her whole body weight landed on that knee every time she leapt.

It's probably nothing, she thought. *It'll sort itself out.*

But as the weeks went on, the pain got worse. From a small twinge, it had become a sharp, shooting pang. Kat was beginning to dread her training sessions. She started taking painkillers before she jumped – but the pain refused to be ignored. Kat couldn't hide her discomfort any longer. She knew she had to tell Mike.

'Kat, you can't keep injuries to yourself!' her coach scolded her. 'You could do lasting damage by training when you're in pain.' He shook his head. Kat was so young. Her body was still developing. 'We need to get you to a specialist.'

Kat grimaced. Her worst fear was that the doctor

would tell her she couldn't jump any more. Her stomach churned with dread. But Mike was right. She couldn't bury her head in the sand. She must pray that her injury wasn't serious...

There was bad news. The doctor diagnosed patellar tendinopathy, also known as Jumper's Knee. 'It's caused by overuse of the patella tendon, just below your knee,' she explained. 'Jumping and landing strains the tendon. It gets gradually damaged. With all the training and competing you do, Katarina, your tendon doesn't have time to repair itself.'

'So what do I do now?' gulped Kat.

'You must rest,' said the doctor. 'No question about it.'

There was horror in Kat's eyes. 'For how long? Can I train?'

'It's going to take months to heal. No jumping. Nothing that puts strain on your knee. You've done serious damage here.'

Kat's eyes filled with tears. No training? No

competitions? While her competitors were working hard, pushing their points tallies upwards, she would be sitting around doing nothing, getting weaker. She could see London 2012 disappearing before her eyes.

The doctor saw her dismay. 'You'll recover, Katarina,' she said gently. 'You can still exercise, but you must be careful.'

Mike nodded. 'We'll make a plan, Kat. You won't be sitting around, don't worry.'

Kat found her injury hard to bear. Without the pressure of jumping every day, the pain in her knee was decreasing. But she missed the thrill of competition, and the weeks of focused training leading up to each one. She missed the camaraderie of her Harriers teammates. She missed the incredible sense of achievement every time she hit a new personal best. She still went to Wavertree, but she felt broken and second-best.

Tracey could see her daughter's unhappiness and did her best to distract her. As the months went by, there were her A-levels to focus on. Going out with her friends. Parties. Football matches. Cuddles with her beloved dachshund, Chorizo. But all Kat wanted was to be well again.

There was one thing that still made Kat smile though: the achievements of her friends. The year 2010 had marked a breakthrough in Jodie's acting career. She had performed professionally onstage for the first time and had been given parts in *Holby City* and *Waterloo Road*. It was completely surreal for Kat, watching her best friend on TV! And while Kat was sad at missing out on the whole of the 2010 athletics season, she was pleased and proud that Jodie was getting the success she deserved. She felt sure that, one day, everyone would know the name Jodie Comer!

* * *

Over a year had passed since Kat's return from injury, and now 2012 had arrived: the year every athlete had been waiting for. The Olympic Games were coming to London in August, and there was just one thing in Kat's thoughts as the training season began: achieving the 5,950 points she needed to qualify for the London 2012 Olympic squad.

Kat hoped to do that at the prestigious Multistars competition held in early May in Desenzano del Garda, Italy. She fondly remembered competing at the World Youth Championships in Bressanon a few years earlier. She loved Italy, with its majestic mountains – and delicious pasta and pizza!

At 19, Kat was the youngest athlete in the Multistars competition. But she and Mike had been working hard on technique, and she was determined to make her mark among the more experienced athletes.

First up was the hurdles. Kat won her heat easily, smashing her personal best. Her time was the second fastest overall. Boom! Second on the leader board!

In the high jump, she cleared 1.81 metres and

retained her position in second. Would her luck hold? The shot put was next, always her weakest event. Kat gritted her teeth, sent a smile towards Tracey who was watching from the stands, and flung herself into the throw. It was another personal best: 11.75 metres!

As if the day couldn't get any better, Kat achieved yet another personal best in the 200 metres, and moved from second place to first. First place on the leader board! Kat could hardly believe it!

She prayed that her good form would continue on the second day of events, and although she ultimately slipped from first position, let down by her performance in the javelin, she still finished in bronze medal position. Competing against a field of older, more experienced athletes, it was a huge achievement. What's more, she had broken Jessica Ennis's British junior record!

But the best thing of all: she had secured a mighty 6,007 points, enough to qualify for the Olympic squad.

Kat could hardly believe it. In just three months, she would be competing at London 2012. Her first Olympics! Between now and August, there would be plenty of hard work, Kat knew. Mike would push her harder than she had ever been pushed before. But right now, she couldn't keep the smile of excitement and pride from her face. The Olympics! It didn't get much bigger than that!

Thank you, Italy, thought Kat. *I love you!*

CHAPTER 10

LONDON CALLING

It was 27 July 2012. As twilight fell over London, a feeling of nervous anticipation swept across the city and the country. The eyes of the world were on the capital and the brand-new Olympic stadium in Stratford. Inside the arena, 80,000 spectators were in their seats, ready to watch the opening ceremony, with many hundreds of millions more watching glued to their TVs across the globe.

'Ladies and gentlemen, welcome to London and to the Games of the thirtieth Olympiad.'

The show that followed was an epic spectacle celebrating the UK, the Commonwealth and the city of London. The crowd watched, mesmerised, as centuries of British history were brought to life by actors, musicians and dancers. Even the Queen played a starring role, performing in a brief sketch with Daniel Craig's James Bond!

Eventually the floodlights went up. It was time for the athletes' parade. Kat watched in wonder as competitors from all 204 Olympic nations streamed into the stadium: athletes, swimmers, cyclists, archers, horse-riders, wrestlers, fencers, gymnasts, boxers... the number was mind-boggling.

This is happening, thought Kat. *This is really happening... and I'm part of it!*

As Team GB, led by the cyclist Chris Hoy, carrying the Union Jack, entered the arena, confetti rained down on them and the crowd went wild. Kat had never heard a sound like it. Her cheeks hurt from smiling, but she couldn't stop. She was brimming with pride to be part of this incredible global celebration of sport!

* * *

The week that followed felt like a month. Kat was longing to be back in the stadium! But finally the big day arrived. Day eight: the start of the athletics events.

Down on the track, Kat looked around her with wide eyes. The stands were bursting with spectators, their excitement brimming over in noisy cheers. Among them was her mum, Tracey, along with the rest of her family. As the TV camera rolled past, Kat smiled and waved, then caught sight of her face projected in epic scale on the big screen. Eek! That would take some getting used to!

On either side of Kat, the athletes sank to their starting blocks, ready for the 100-metres hurdles. An electric tension filled the air, finally cut through by the bang of the starting gun and the roar of the crowd. Kat darted from the blocks. From now on, every microsecond was a series of calculations.

The length of her stride. The angle of her body approaching the hurdle. The position of her feet as they took off and landed. She channelled every ounce of power, speed and precision into these movements.

Seconds later, Kat raced across the finish line, behind a handful of more experienced athletes. Was it fast? It had *felt* fast.

The results appeared almost immediately on the huge electronic screen. More cheers. Kat was fourth in her heat. With a time of 13.48 seconds, she had equalled her personal best!

Giving each other hugs and pats on the back, the athletes left the track. They were all aware that it was the next heat, heat five, that the spectators were *really* waiting for. This was the race Jess was running in: Jessica Ennis, the best heptathlete the country had ever known, Great Britain's gold medal hopeful. Kat held her breath. She felt almost as nervous as if she were running the race herself!

If the noise had been extraordinary before,

now it was out of this world. A shiver went down Kat's spine. The expectation of every single British supporter was on Jess's shoulders. But there was also support and adoration. Jess was a hero.

They were off!

Kat didn't take her eyes from the 26-year-old as she rocketed from hurdle to hurdle, crossing the line in first place with a huge grin on her face. The crowd had hoped for a sparkling performance – and Jess had delivered.

But how fast had it been?

Kat's eyes flew to the big screen. A world record! The crowd were on their feet, a sea of red, white and blue. Kat's heart thumped with pride. Jess deserved this moment and the stadium reverberated with sheer, unbridled joy.

One event down, six to go!

Next up was the high jump, Kat's best event. *The crowd will have calmed down by now*, she thought. *They'll be waiting for Jess again. They won't be interested in my jump.*

But she was wrong. Even before she began her run-up, the crowd were clapping her: a slow, steady handclap, like a chant, ringing through the stadium. They were with her – this huge stadium crowd was right behind her, willing her to succeed!

Kat's surprise turned to adrenaline. She felt it surge through her legs as she sauntered into her run-up. When she took her jump, it felt like flying.

There was a wild eruption of cheers as she soared over the crossbar – 1.89 metres. Kat's hands flew to her face. She couldn't believe it: a personal best in her first Olympic high jump, in front of a cheering home crowd.

A huge smile broke onto Kat's face. This was surreal. Utterly surreal. A moment she would cherish forever.

The shot put and 200 metres followed, and day one of the heptathlon was finally over. Kat was in fourteenth place on the leader board. Jess was leading, in gold medal position.

The sun had set over London by the time Kat

arrived back in the Olympic Village. Once again a grin broke over her face. This small pocket of east London was home, for one extraordinary month, to over 10,000 athletes from 204 countries. How amazing it felt to be part of this huge international community! Athletes were strolling in and out of the accommodation blocks, laughing and talking, exploring their new home. A hubbub was coming from the vast dining hall where hundreds – no, thousands – of athletes were sitting at the long tables, eating, laughing and talking. The whole village was buzzing with fun and laughter and camaraderie.

How different it will be, thought Kat, *when the competition begins again tomorrow!*

CHAPTER 11

SUPER SATURDAY

The next day, Saturday, dawned bright. Kat felt refreshed as she strode into the stadium for her fourth event, the long jump. She gave another strong performance and the crowd cheered their enthusiastic support.

But, once again, it was Jess who led the field. Her performances had been flawless. Every time she entered the arena, she was greeted with cheers of wild delight. By the end of the day, with just one event to go – the 800 metres – the gold medal was firmly in her grasp. Jess had only to finish the race and she would be crowned Olympic champion.

The hopes of a nation rode on her shoulders!

First, though, it was Kat's turn to race. She was 16th on the leader board. As she took her place on the start line for her heat, she beamed for the TV cameras. She had loved every single magical moment of these two days, and the audience could see it shining in her face.

As the starting gun fired, Kat was quickly overtaken by the more experienced competitors. The pace was fast, but Kat was keeping up. She remained close at the back of the leading group as they completed the first lap. But Kat knew she had more to give. With 50 metres to go, she began to propel herself forward. Urging her tired legs faster, she overtook first one, then two, then three runners. Her heart was thumping as she powered across the line in second place. She had given her all.

With a time of 2 minutes and 10.76 seconds, she had smashed her personal best!

But before Kat could find out her overall ranking, there was the final. All eyes, including Kat's, were on Jessica Ennis. Kat watched as Jess pulled sharply away, leading the field for the first 500 metres. But with 300 metres to go, three runners edged past her, led by the world champion, Tatyana Chernova.

Kat's heart was in her mouth. *Come on, Jess! Come on!* She had seen her teammate fight back many times before. So had the crowd. Their confidence in her was total. *Come on, Jess!*

They were rewarded.

Approaching the final 100 metres, Jess rocketed forward. When she finally crossed the line, it was with a clear lead, her arms held victoriously in the air. Not only was she the winner but she had also set an incredible new world record!

Kat whooped for joy. It was exactly the finish that she, the crowd, and the nation, had hoped for. Great Britain's first athletics gold of the Olympics! Her heart went out to her brilliant, talented, hard-working teammate. Watching Jess was an inspiration. Would she, Kat, one day taste the glory that Jess was enjoying?

As she ran back onto the track to embrace the heptathlon queen, Kat knew she would do everything in her power to deserve future Olympic glory as much as Jess did right now!

* * *

Kat's final score was 6,267 points, placing her fifteenth out of thirty heptathletes overall. Friends, family, coaches, commentators... everyone agreed that it was a brilliant achievement for such a young athlete. At just 19, Kat had been the youngest in the squad. Destined for greatness? The next Jessica Ennis? A lot of people seemed to think so!

Back in Liverpool, Tracey, Jodie and her rest of her friends celebrated Kat's Olympic achievement with as much energy as Kat had put into her 800 metres. Kat glowed with pride. It was almost like she'd won a medal herself!

The Olympics marked the end of the season. Finally, it was time to relax. Kat's next stop that summer was the Bahamas. Throughout her childhood, she and Tracey had made regular trips to visit Ricky, but as a teenager, with the pressure of training, Kat hadn't seen so much of her dad.

Ricky was bubbling with joy to see his Olympian daughter and, it turned out, so was the rest of the country. The Bahamas had their own national team, of course, but they were also on Team Katarina.

'Watch this, Kat,' said Ricky. 'I recorded it for you. I think you'll like it.'

He flicked on the TV. On the screen, Kat saw herself in the Olympic stadium, preparing for her day-one high jump. As the crowd in London clapped along, the Bahamian commentator introduced her with as much pride and excitement as if she'd been a homegrown athlete:

'Our girl, Katarina Johnson-Thompson...'

'Dad, that's amazing!' Katarina felt like crying. It gave her a warm glow inside to think that here, over four thousand miles away, she had as much support as she had back in Liverpool.

'You're one of us,' Ricky said, smiling. 'Never forget, you belong here too.'

And the sunny Bahamas really did feel like home to Kat. Everywhere they went, she was welcomed like one of the family. It was clear to Kat that Ricky talked about her to his friends and neighbours all the time!

'You'll have to stop it, Dad,' she joked. 'People will be so disappointed when they meet me and find out how normal I am.'

'Impossible!' Ricky pulled her into a hug. 'I'm so proud of you, my beautiful girl. Isn't it lucky your mother let you give up ballet lessons!'

They both dissolved into giggles. The days of dance classes, leotards and ballet shoes felt so long ago!

'Mum's become the biggest sports fan ever,' smiled Kat. 'She gets so nervous though. It almost makes me nervous.'

Ricky grinned. 'She's invested.'

'I wish she'd chill out a bit sometimes!' Kat laughed.

* * *

It was soon time for Kat to swap the beautiful beaches of Nassau for a busy training season. Her next international event would be in August 2013 – the 2013 IAAF World Championships heptathlon in Moscow. It was only her second ever senior championship. Her target? To finish in the top eight.

Kat had taken her A-levels the previous year and had begun a degree in Sports Science at Liverpool John Moores University. In a whirl of training, studying, and more training, August and the world championships came round very quickly.

All British hopes were riding on Kat this time. Jess – now Jess Ennis-Hill, following her wedding earlier in the year – was out of action with a muscle injury. Tracey watched from the stand, swallowing her nerves as Kat ran, jumped and threw. By the end of day two, the tension was nail-biting. With only the 800 metres to go, there were seven athletes with enough points to win bronze – Kat among them.

Cheered on by Tracey, Kat ran her fastest 800 metres ever. It was an epic performance, but not quite enough to take her into bronze medal position. She finished in fifth with 6,449, a personal best, 28 points behind the bronze medallist, Dafne Schippers from the Netherlands.

Kat was delighted with her performance. But a question was gnawing at her. Had her ambitions been too modest? She had easily made the top eight. Should she be aiming for international medals now? That bronze had been tantalisingly close...

She sighed. There was one big thing that was holding her back: those tricksy throws. In the shot put, she had finished a disappointing 31st out of 33 competitors. She would have to improve if she wanted to claim a medal next time.

***

Kat didn't have too long to wait till the next international competition. Apart from the annual

KATARINA JOHNSON-THOMPSON

world championships, the biggest event in the multi-event calendar was the Hypo-Meeting in Götzis, Austria in May. Past winners included a 'who's who' of Kat's greatest heroes, from Daley Thompson in the men's decathlon to Denise Lewis and Jessica Ennis in the heptathlon.

Jess wouldn't be competing in 2014. She was pregnant with her first child. So, once again, everyone was watching Kat.

Kat rose to the occasion and shone. She set a personal best in the javelin, won the long jump and stormed to victory in the 800 metres. Even Tracey's nervous text messages couldn't put her off! This time, she was a medallist. A gold medallist! Kat received her honour with a smile that lit up the stadium.

Next up, in July, would be the Commonwealth Games in Glasgow.

And this time, Kat was the favourite.

CHAPTER 12

PRESSURE

'Ta-da!' With a flourish, Tracey unfurled her masterpiece. 'What do you think, Kat?'

Kat let out a peal of surprised laughter. 'A banner! It's brilliant, Mum!'

Tracey smiled. 'Eye-catching, isn't it?'

Several metres in length, with huge letters spelling out Kat's double-barrelled name, the banner was going to be unmissable.

'Wow, my name really is a mouthful, isn't it? This is so thoughtful, Mum, thank you.'

'It's your first Commonwealth Games,' Tracey smiled. 'We had to do something special!'

Kat visualised herself in the arena, catching sight of the humongous banner. She grinned. 'I love it. And I'm glad you're all coming to watch.'

This time, the whole extended family would be there in the stadium. Tracey had hired a minibus to take everyone to Glasgow where they would stay for a week and soak up the atmosphere of the Games, as well as being there to cheer Kat on in her seven events.

'We wouldn't miss it for the world,' said Tracey. 'Your nan's so excited.'

***

With a little over a week to go before the Games, Kat's final training was going perfectly to plan. Kat was working hard and Mike was full of encouragement. He knew, now Kat had tasted gold at Götzis, that she was hungry to be on the podium again. Mike, like everyone else, was optimistic that this would be Kat's competition.

Just a few days before the event, Kat was at Wavertree as usual. Mike was surprised to hear Kat calling out to him from a bench at the side of the training hall.

'I–I can't feel my foot. I think it's cramp.'

Mike ran over. Kat's left foot, her take-off foot, was badly swollen. Her face was full of anxiety. 'I can't put weight on it. Look, I can't even get my trainer on.'

Mike frowned. So close to a major competition, an injury like this was very bad news. 'We won't do any more training today,' he said. 'Go home and let me know how it feels in the morning.'

He helped Kat to hobble outside and into a taxi. 'Hopefully it'll be back to normal in a few hours,' he told her.

Kat braved a smile. 'It's already feeling a bit better. Fingers crossed.'

The pain soon went away and Kat went to bed relieved. But the next morning, the discomfort returned. Kat rang Mike and they went straight to the physio, who recommended a scan.

Once the scan came back, the answer was clear.

'It's a stress-fracture,' the physio reported. 'Tiny – but that's where the pain is coming from. It'll only get worse if you jump on it before it's healed. You could do long-term damage.'

Kat looked at Mike. He shook his head. 'There isn't enough time. Not for the Commonwealths.'

Kat let out a sob of dismay. Her first Commonwealth Games. She wanted desperately to compete in front of a home crowd. How disappointed her family would be! And Tracey's banner – it would go to waste! Tears trickled down Kat's cheeks. 'I can't believe I'm going to miss out,' she whispered. 'It's not fair.'

'We'll focus on the Europeans,' said Mike. 'Hopefully you'll be fit again by then.'

But by the time the European Championships came around in August, Kat's fracture still wasn't fully healed. Seven events wouldn't be possible, not with an injury, but could she enter the individual long jump? She couldn't bear the thought of missing the competition entirely!

Mike remained cautious. 'It's too risky,' he told her. 'We need you fully fit before you compete in any event.'

* * *

Missing out on two major championships was the hardest challenge Kat had faced so far. Sitting on the sidelines was so tough. Every week when she wasn't competing felt like a year. She couldn't shake the fear that her body simply wasn't strong enough for the seven gruelling events of the heptathlon. Now when she trained, she thought less about pushing herself and more about not getting hurt. Her self-belief was crumbling.

All that kept her going was the thought of Liverpool FC and their extraordinary 2005 UEFA Champions League Final. If they could pull through so could she. With the support of Tracey and her friends, Kat gritted her teeth and did battle against self-doubt. She trained as much as she could. She took care not to push herself too hard. Slowly her strength and determination gradually came creeping back.

And whenever she needed cheering up, there was one thing guaranteed to make her smile.

CHAPTER 13

BRONX AND CHORIZO

'Oh, I hope they'll get on okay!'

Kat wore a nervous expression on her face. In her arms, she held a tiny brown sausage-shaped creature, squirming to be released.

'Chorizo,' she said, addressing the handsome dachshund who sat on the ground in front of her. 'This is Bronx. Be nice to him!'

Chorizo had been part of the family for several years. How was he going to react to a new arrival? Kat placed the puppy on to the floor. The two dogs took a cautious step towards one another, before the younger dog, Bronx, launched into a bouncing, whirling frenzy, tearing wildly round the older dog before rushing off to explore the room.

Kat turned to Tracey. 'Well, someone's happy!'

'He's adorable!' smiled Tracey.

Chorizo watched Bronx in confusion for a moment before following him, tail wagging, on a tour of the room.

'You realise he's going to chew *everything*, don't you?' Tracey warned. They were in the living room of Kat's new house. 'Nothing will be safe any more.'

Kat laughed. 'I don't mind! As long as he doesn't chew Chorizo's tennis ball. That will cause trouble.'

But, of course, the puppy made a beeline for Chorizo's beloved tennis ball as soon as he spotted it. Chorizo turned to stare at Kat with horror in his big brown eyes.

Kat stroked her dog's head. 'Don't worry, Chorizo, his mouth is too tiny. Look!' The tennis ball was bigger than Bronx's head. His whole body was barely bigger than a banana.

'Oh, he's the cutest thing.' Tracey bent down to

tickle Bronx as he scampered past. He responded by rolling on to his back, kicking his short legs frantically in the air. 'Will he calm down as he gets older, I wonder?'

'I hope not,' grinned Kat, and Tracey laughed. How good it was to see her daughter smiling again!

By the end of the day, the two dogs were happily curled up, side by side, in Chorizo's basket. Kat let out a sigh of relief. How awful it would be if the dogs hadn't become friends.

'I've taken a million pictures,' she said, waving her phone.

Chorizo already had his own Instagram account. Bronx would be a photogenic new addition. How cute they were together!

Tiny Bronx was fearless too. By the end of the week, he could wrestle a toy from Chorizo's mouth. Chorizo's dinner wasn't safe either.

'That dog needs some training,' said Tracey.

'Already sorted,' said Kat. Her packed schedule now included weekly puppy training classes. 'We start tomorrow!'

But excitable Bronx was slow to grasp the idea of training. Sit? Stay? There was just too much to explore! And once he was off, he was off...

'Bronx! Bronx! Come here!' called Kat. 'All the other puppies can do this now. Come back!' Finally Kat gave in and chased after her runaway sausage dog. 'Bronx – focus, please. You're letting us down.'

Kat's competitive spirit was kicking in. She was determined that Bronx would succeed.

'We're going to get it right,' she insisted, fondling his velvety ears. 'We're going to practise all this at home.'

By the end of the year, Bronx's training still had a way to go. But Kat herself was fully fit again, and ready to start competing. She was determined to make 2015 her best year yet.

And she began it in style...

In February, she jumped a spectacular 1.97 metres to break the British high jump record at the British Indoor Championships in Sheffield.

A week later, she set a new indoor long jump record at the Birmingham Indoor Grand Prix: a stunning 6.93 metres.

Then, in March, at the 2015 European Indoor Championships in Prague, she broke the British pentathlon record.

'See, Bronx – what you can achieve with a bit of focus,' she laughed.

Kat's eyes were on the World Championships in Beijing later in the year – and after that, the Rio Olympics in 2016. Her goal was to exceed two metres for the high jump and more than seven metres for the long jump. And, of course, there were her other five events to prepare for as well. Kat's training schedule looked like a school timetable, with sessions in every discipline, plus hill runs and weights training.

Even when she wasn't on the track or field at Wavertree or Manchester, Kat was thinking about her performance. As Beijing drew near, Mike encouraged her to visualise each event in turn, to picture what might go wrong and how she could overcome it. As she lay in bed, the whole heptathlon would play out in her mind. On a good day, she would see victory.

Her mantra? *Run faster, sprint harder, fly higher, do yourself justice!*

CHAPTER 14

GREAT
EXPECTATIONS

From her viewing point, Kat gazed with wide eyes at the city of Beijing stretched out below. Weird and wonderfully shaped skyscrapers towered up towards the sky, while on the ground, tangles of glittering highway wound through the city. Dominating the view was the Chinese National Stadium, known as the Bird's Nest, its interior lit with fiery orange and gold.

Kat was in Beijing for the 2015 World Championships. It was only her second World Championships, following Moscow two years earlier. Back then she had set herself a modest target and exceeded it. With Jessica Ennis-Hill only just back in competition after giving birth to her little boy, Reggie, this time Kat was the favourite to win.

In just a few months, everything had changed for Kat. The interview requests had begun to arrive, from newspapers, magazines, blogs. She was quizzed about her training regime, what she ate, what she wore. She thought back to when she was 19 and people had started calling her the next Jessica Ennis. Then, it had felt like a joke. Now, it felt very real. She could feel the pressure weighing down on her, pressing in on either side.

Kat blinked. The expectations, the pressure, it all felt as surreal as the view. Thrilling but scary.

The big question... Was she ready?

***

A familiar feeling of nerves and elation swept over Kat as she stepped into the Bird's Nest stadium the next morning. The day started well. She finished a respectable third place in the hurdles – Jess's strongest event – but beat the Olympic champion in the 200 metres and high jump. She was 13th in the shot put – but she had become used to losing points in the throwing events and compensating for them with her strong running and jumping.

At the end of the first day, Kat was second on the leader board, behind Jess in first place.

Silver medal position. So far, so good!

The second day had two of Kat's strongest events: the long jump and the 800 metres. She knew she could beat Jess with ease when it came to jumping.

First up was the long jump. Kat trained her eyes on the sand pit. Each fibre of her body knew what to do. She flew along the run-up and propelled her weight onto her left leg. Then she was up, soaring over the pit. In her head, she told herself: *Don't land, don't land, don't land...*

Finally Kat tumbled down into the sand. She sprang straight back up, eager to know her distance. But, no one was clapping. No one was cheering.

There was silence and... a red flag!

Kat's heart sank. A red flag meant a foul. Her take-off foot must have overstepped the take-off line and hit the plasticine board behind it. The long jump rules were strict and the officials were watching the line on a screen.

She walked back to the other end of the run-up, gearing herself up for her second attempt. *Play it safe*, she told herself.

She sprinted and leapt into the jump, cautiously this time, mentally measuring the distance as she placed her foot for take-off.

But – another foul. Surely not! Kat shook her head in despair. She had one more chance left. In a split second she decided to go for it – to aim for a big jump and not hold back. She rocketed along the runway, legs and arms pumping, then – she was up! She kicked vigorously in mid-air, propelling herself forward before plunging back down to earth.

It was a huge jump! Getting up out of the sand, she clenched her hands into fists, beaming with delight. Finally! But – wait... the officials were crowding round the take-off board again. The red flag hadn't been raised – what was going on?

Anxiety flooded into Kat's head. She joined the group bending over the board. A jumper's foot was allowed to touch the plastic covering of the board, as long as it didn't make an indent in the plasticine underneath. Surely she had just grazed the plastic? There hadn't been any pressure?

'Check. Can you please check?' she pleaded.

While the officials removed the board from its position and examined it, Kat hurried to the sidelines where Mike was watching every move.

'You're doing the right thing,' he told her. 'If there is any doubt, always argue the case. Clearly there is doubt or they would simply have raised the flag.'

'I didn't feel my foot touch the board.' Kat's face was all confusion. 'I'm sure I didn't.'

The wait was unbearable. Had her left foot scuffed the plasticine? Had she made an imprint?

Finally an official raised the red flag. On to the screen flashed the dreaded decision: three Xs. Three fouls. Kat would get no points for the long jump.

It was over. There would be no medal for her in Beijing. Unless her competitors had similar bad luck, she would finish at the very bottom of the leader board.

Kat's shoulders slumped in dismay and her eyes welled with tears. Jess appeared next to her, having just completed her own jump. She put her arms round her teammate.

'I know how you're feeling,' she whispered. 'It's awful to lose out this way.'

There were still two events to go. Kat had to carry on. Despite knowing she would come bottom, or close to it, she wouldn't be allowed to pull out. Unless they were injured, all the heptathletes had to finish the competition.

With the javelin out of the way, it was time for the 800 metres, the final event. Kat and Mike had agreed a strategy: she would get through it with minimal effort. She would save her energy to compete in the individual long jump event a few days later. Perhaps she would be able to salvage some Beijing glory that way.

Now that she was at the bottom of the leader board, Kat's heat contained the weakest competitors. She could have beaten them easily if she was trying. But she wasn't. She let the other racers leave her far behind. At the end of the two laps, Kat trailed across the line in last position and barely out of breath. She felt sad and, worse, she felt ashamed. She had let everyone down. Herself, her mum, Mike, her fans.

At the side of the track, Phil Jones from BBC Sport was waiting to interview her. She walked slowly over to the camera and Phil held out the mic.

'That must have been tough,' he said.

Kat mustered a smile. 'It's been a disappointing day,' she said. And, blinking back tears, she described her frustration at the horrible long jump result.

'But I know we're going to see plenty more from you,' Phil said encouragingly.

As soon as the mic was switched off, Kat's tears began to fall. She didn't care that she was probably still being filmed. There were cameras everywhere at the World Championships. The tears kept coming and coming.

Shortly afterwards, Kat sat on the sidelines and watched Jess triumph in the 800 metres final to win the gold medal. One thing was for sure – as heartbroken as she was, Kat couldn't begrudge her teammate her victory. Jess had worked so hard to get fit again after having a baby. She was a worthy winner.

But while Jess savoured her victory, Kat's confidence was shattered. She had finished in twenty-eighth position. How was she ever going to come back from this?

CHAPTER 15

ROAD TO RIO

Kat was back in Liverpool. Surrounding her were her loving friends and family, plus the snuggly, adorable duo of Bronx and Chorizo. She was back in training, doing the events that she loved. But the joy had gone out of it. The smile had left her face.

'You have to learn to move on, Kat,' Mike told her. 'You have huge talent. A bad day is just a bad day. Nothing more.'

Kat gave a little smile. She knew all about bad days. So much could go wrong in the heptathlon.

'I'm trying,' she murmured.

But Mike had a nagging feeling that there was something more to Kat's gloom. 'It's the pressure, isn't it?'

Kat nodded. She wasn't used to the spotlight. She had always been in the background while Jess shouldered the public expectation. Before, she had been competing for herself. It was so different now that everyone expected amazing things of her. When she didn't succeed, there were journalists writing about it, online trolls telling her she was a failure.

'It's too much,' she said quietly. 'There are so many people saying things about me. I just want it to stop.'

Mike sighed. Everyone could see Kat's talent. But she was still so young, only 21. She hadn't yet developed fully as an athlete. If only people could understand that!

'You have plenty of time,' he said. 'Move on. Shut everything else out. You have to, Kat.'

But try as she might, Kat couldn't put Beijing out

of her mind. She had worked so hard – only for it all to come crumbling down! When she visualised the next championship, she could see only failure.

'We need to focus on Olympic qualification,' Mike reminded her. 'Décastar is the next challenge.'

The Décastar event in Talence, France, in September 2015, was Kat's next opportunity to secure the points she needed to qualify for the Rio Olympics. She summoned her strength and her positivity. She had bounced back before. She could do it again.

By the time she arrived in France, it seemed to be working. At the end of day one, she led the field. With the nerve-wracking hurdles and the dreaded shot put out of the way, she went into day two feeling confident. She added a strong 200 metres to her success. With just two more events to go, she was feeling good.

The javelin had never been Kat's strong point, but she had been receiving special coaching from Goldie Sayers, the leading British javelin thrower.

Kat had been visualising her throw for weeks before the competition: memorising every step of the run-up, the angle of her body and her arm as she flung the javelin and watched it arc through the air...

Now she just needed to make it a reality.

But as she launched into the run-up, her thigh muscle gave a sharp twinge. *Focus*, she told herself. *Ignore the pain. Throw.*

She flung her body into the throw, before crumpling with pain as the javelin left her hand. Her score: a disappointing 29.15 metres.

Kat limped to the sidelines and her physio rushed over.

'You've pulled your adductor,' he said.

Kat grimaced. The pain in her leg was agonising; she was lucky to have managed the throw at all.

'My knee is hurting too,' she said. 'The left one. Even more than usual.'

The physio frowned. He knew Kat's history, the patellar tendinopathy she had suffered a few years earlier. Kat had had regular knee issues ever since, and she often took painkillers before she jumped. 'You won't be able to run the 800 metres,' he said. 'No way.'

Kat put her head in her hands. Her mind flashed back to Beijing and that horrible long jump. Another competition over! Another failure! She couldn't believe it.

There was one silver lining though: even without the 800 metre race, she had secured enough points to qualify for Rio.

If I'm fit enough to compete, that is, she thought gloomily.

* * *

Kat's medical team sprang into action as soon as she was back in Liverpool. The adductor would heal itself with rest and care. Her left knee was a bigger problem though. Scans showed a bone growth in her knee that was pushing into her tendon. Kat needed an operation.

To an athlete, 'operation' is the most horrific word in the dictionary. Kat fought back a tidal wave of fears. Would it go well? Would she recover successfully? Would she still be competing at the same level afterwards?

Tracey tried to reassure her. 'Of course it'll go well, love,' she said. 'You'll be fit again in no time.'

But the kind words of friends and family couldn't soothe Kat's anxiety. 'I'm falling apart, Mum,' she cried. 'The heptathlon is breaking me. I'm not sure I'm strong enough for this.'

'Every athlete gets injured,' Tracey said. 'You're doing one of the toughest sports there is. Even as a dancer, I got injured. But I always came back. Always. And you will too.'

Kat summoned a smile. She knew she had inherited some of her mum's stubbornness. Setbacks were tough to deal with, but deep down she knew she would never give up.

'Thanks, Mum,' she said.

'I believe in you, sweetheart,' said Tracey, holding her close. 'I believe you're destined for great things. You've already achieved so much.'

Hobbling around on crutches after her operation, Kat's achievements felt very far away to her. But she thought about the 2005 UEFA Champions League Final between AC Milan and her beloved Liverpool. *Never rule out the underdog. She might be injured. She might be down. But she would come back fighting.*

So she channelled every bit of determination into her recovery, into getting back to Wavertree, getting fit, getting back into competition.

But something was missing. Everyone could see it. With a pang of sorrow, Tracey realised that her daughter didn't smile any more. She didn't smile on the track. She didn't smile in training.

Would Rio put the spring back into Kat's step? The smile back on her face? Her mum prayed every day that it would.

CHAPTER 16

HAVE FAITH

In his apartment in Nassau, Ricky Thompson was glued to the TV and the coverage of the 2016 Rio Olympics. He had already watched his daughter compete in the 100 metres. Her time, 13.48 seconds, was 'disappointing', according to the commentators, but in Ricky's eyes, Katarina was already a winner. He didn't see his daughter often these days, but she was always in his heart and he was brimming with pride for her. His apartment was full of photos and newspaper and magazine cuttings, celebrating her success.

It was time for the high jump, Kat's best event.

Ricky leapt up from his chair, flung his front door open and called into the street. 'It's my daughter's high jump. Katarina is about to jump. Our girl, Katarina! Come and watch! Quickly!'

Everyone in Nassau knew Kat's name. Soon there was a large group of spectators – friends, neighbours and strangers alike – piled into Ricky's living room. On the TV, the stadium crowd hushed as Kat began her run-up. Ricky could barely contain his excitement. He whispered the little prayer that he always spoke before she competed. *God protect her. Make her strong.*

It was as if Kat had a jetpack on her shoulders as she sprinted down the runway. Ricky had never seen her run so fast. He could see the concentration on her face, the focus in her eyes. From her left leg, she launched into a turbo-powered jump, twisting in mid-air and flipping on to her back to curl gracefully over the crossbar. The bar was steady, showing no sign of toppling. It was 1.98 metres, a personal best!

The crowd in the arena cheered with appreciation. Ricky leapt to his feet, flinging his arms into the air. 'Katarina! My girl!' He whirled around the room, clapping his new friends on the back, shaking hands and giving hugs. 'That's my Katarina!' he cried. 'She's going to win gold! I tell you. She's going to win this.'

It was a stunning performance. But, 6,000 miles away, in the Maracanã stadium in Rio de Janeiro, Kat struggled to share her dad's delight. She knew by now that a great performance in one event wasn't nearly enough to win the heptathlon. Even with this huge jump behind her, anything could still go wrong.

The truth was, Kat didn't want to be here in Rio. The fear of another injury was constantly in her mind. Old injuries were causing her discomfort. Her self-belief was at rock bottom.

She longed to be back home in Liverpool, safely away from the spotlight, away from the pressure and expectation. When she tried to visualise standing on the Olympic podium, receiving a medal, she couldn't. If only she could flick a switch and turn off the endless stream of worry and doubt!

By the end of day one, Kat was too far down the leader board to be a medal contender. Once again, it was Jess who was excelling. She was in silver medal position, exceeding every expectation, while a young Belgian athlete, Nafissatou Thiam, was in gold medal position. Nafi was two years younger than Kat, new to international competition, and brimming with talent. Hope, ambition and excitement shone from her face.

I used to feel like that, thought Kat to herself. *Now I'm just disappointing everyone.*

Kat dreaded the start of day two. As she went from event to event, a day had never felt so long. Finally, it was time for the 800 metres, the last event. Night had fallen over Rio; the athletes would run in the bright glare of the floodlights. Usually Kat loved to run at night. The glow of the stadium lights was thrilling. But tonight she felt flat. Her legs felt heavy. She wished she were anywhere but here. Anywhere at all.

Only the thought of how much her family and friends, in Liverpool and Nassau, loved and supported her, gave her the boost she needed. The 800 metres was one of her strongest races. She would go out there and do her best.

The starting gun fired. The runners were away. As the group picked up speed, Kat propelled herself into fifth position. Jess was in the lead, with Nafissatou Thiam trailing at the back of the group. As they went into the second lap, Kat powered into fourth place. She dug deep, tried to find the energy to propel herself forward into third, but the two runners ahead of her still had more to give. They sped away, racing each other to the finish line, leaving Kat far behind.

In a matter of seconds, the points had been calculated to give the athlete's overall scores. Despite a disappointing performance in the 800 metres, the talented newcomer Nafi Thiam had taken the gold medal. Jess had won silver. Kat trailed behind in sixth place.

If this had been four years ago, back at London 2012, Kat would have been thrilled at coming sixth out of thirty. But right here, right now, with world championship glory behind her, it was a huge blow. As the finalists, led by Nafi, circled the track together for their victory lap, Kat's face couldn't hide her misery.

Jess jogged over to her and they ran side by side. 'Kat, are you okay?' she asked.

'It's hopeless,' Kat whispered. 'I've let everyone down. I don't think I want to do this any more.'

Jess's eyes filled with pity. 'I've been there,' she said. 'We've all had highs and lows. When you're down, you need to keep believing that the next success is just around the corner.'

It felt to Kat as though there had been nothing but lows, setback after setback. 'All I'm doing is failing, Jess. What if I'm just not good enough?'

'You are,' Jess insisted. 'You're so talented,

Kat. You have to have faith that it'll all come together eventually.'

Jess knew there wasn't much she could say to comfort her teammate. She could see Kat's confidence was shattered once again. If only Kat could see that setbacks were there to make her stronger.

'I believe in you, Kat. You need to believe in yourself.'

CHAPTER 17

BROKEN

Mike was worried. Back in training in Liverpool, Kat was suffering injury after injury. He could see anxiety written all over her face. Her confidence had never been so low.

Something had to be done. Something had to change, and he made up his mind to speak to her.

'I've been thinking, Kat. High jump has always been your biggest strength, hasn't it? If you had been competing in the individual high jump in Rio, rather than heptathlon, your jump would have won you the gold. I think you should focus on that from now on. Become a high jumper.'

Kat blinked. She stared at him blankly. 'And give up the heptathlon?'

Mike nodded. 'One event rather than seven will put much less strain on your body. You won't get injured as much. You'll be able to relax a little.'

Kat's face broke into a frown. 'But I love the heptathlon.'

'You *used* to love it,' Mike said, shaking his head. 'I don't think you've loved it for over a year.'

Kat couldn't disagree with this. On the track in Rio, she had wanted to give up. But hearing the idea from someone else, a spark of stubbornness flared up inside her. 'I want to keep going, Mike. I still have more to offer. I'm sure of it. I don't want to give up.'

'It wouldn't be giving up, Kat. It would be refocusing your energy. Please think about it.'

Kat nodded. She knew as well as Mike did that things couldn't go on as they were. But she also knew that giving up the heptathlon wasn't the answer. There had to be another way.

And she was determined to find it.

* * *

By September, Kat had come up with an answer.

It was a risk.

It was scary.

It meant leaving behind everything she knew, everything that was familiar.

She needed a new coach.

Kat was so grateful for everything Mike had done for her. He had taught her all she knew. But it was time to move on, to push herself in different ways.

Mike understood. 'I'll always be wishing the best for you, Kat. You deserve huge success.'

Kat smiled and gave him a hug. 'Thank you so much. I hope my next coach is as brilliant as you are.'

But who would that next coach be?

Kat felt a mix of excitement and nerves as she began her search. Luckily, she had some expert help, from none other than former heptathlete and Olympic medallist Denise Lewis. If anyone could help her find the perfect coach, it was Denise.

'You may have to travel to find the right person, Kat,' warned Denise. 'First I want to take you to Amsterdam to meet Charles van Commenee. He was my coach while I was competing.'

Kat nodded. 'Yes, please.'

So together they travelled to the Netherlands and watched Charles as he led a training session with his team. Kat admired how driven he was. He and Denise had had a great relationship.

'I don't think he's the right coach for me though,' she admitted.

'We've only just started,' smiled Denise. 'There are a lot of people still to meet. I have a list!'

So, slowly but surely, they worked their way through the list, meeting coaches all over Europe. How interesting it was to see other coaches in action, to observe their techniques. She tried to imagine herself being trained by each of them. Would they push her? Would they support her? Would she have fun?

There were so many different styles, techniques and personalities. If only she wasn't so indecisive!

'Next we're going to Montpellier to see Jean-Yves Cochand,' Denise announced. Jean-Yves was a former athlete, who had been coaching athletics since Denise was a junior.

Kat recognised his name instantly. 'He's a legend!'

'Jean-Yves will be retiring soon,' Denise told her, 'but I'd like him to see you perform. His advice will be worthwhile, I promise you.'

'I hope so,' sighed Kat. They had met so many coaches and she was longing to find the right person and get to work.

* * *

'Katarina, you will never win a medal if you throw like that!'

Kat grimaced. Oh dear! Jean-Yves was one of the best coaches in the world. If he said her shot put was bad, it was bad. She hardly dared pick up the javelin now; she was scared of his brutal honesty!

'All wrong,' was Jean-Yves' verdict as she hurled the javelin into the throwing circle. 'Wrong – but you can fix it. Oh, yes, you can definitely fix it, if you work hard.'

Phew! That was all Kat needed to hear. She needed to know she was capable of improving, and Jean-Yves let her know that.

'I'll give it everything!' she said.

Jean-Yves nodded. 'I can see that. Stay here in Montpellier a few days, Katarina. That way we'll see if we can work together.'

Kat looked across at Denise and a smile spread across her face. For the first time in months, she felt hopeful and happy. She felt sure that Jean-Yves would be able to help her. His confidence and his honesty had inspired her. Denise grinned back. They were both thinking the same thing: *this could be it!*

Kat's stay in Montpellier was a success. She

enjoyed being out on the track with Jean-Yves and his colleague, Bertrand Valcin, who would be her main coach if she decided to stay. She ran and threw and jumped and was warmly welcomed by the French athletes who were also coached by Bertrand: Olympic decathlon medallist Kevin Mayer and European heptathlon champion Antoinette Nana Djimou.

With the bright Mediterranean skies above her, Kat was beginning to enjoy herself again. And for once, she didn't struggle with indecision. Her mind was made up. 'I want to train here in Montpellier!'

CHAPTER 18

FRENCH ADVENTURE

It was tough to say goodbye to friends and family and move to a different country, but Kat felt sure she was doing the right thing. Tracey was sad to see her daughter leave Liverpool. However, she could see the sparkle returning to Kat's eyes.

'It's going to be an adventure,' she told her. 'I'll support you whatever you do.'

'I'll call you lots,' Kat promised. 'And I'll be back in Liverpool plenty.'

Tracey wasn't the only one who would miss Kat. Bronx and Chorizo stared up at her with sad puppy-dog eyes as she prepared to leave. Why were there so many suitcases? Where was she going? When would she be back?

'Oh, Bronx, Chorizo, don't make this difficult!' Kat cried. She knew how much she was going to miss them. 'I'll be back to cuddle you soon, I promise. In the meantime, be good for your grandmother!'

* * *

Kat soon fell in love with elegant Montpellier. She enjoyed getting lost in the maze of narrow streets, filled with interesting shops and delicious-looking bakeries. There was the magnificent Arc de Triomphe, the bustling Place de la Comédie, and the towering St Peter's Cathedral, all made of the same warm golden stone. And beyond the city was the glittering Mediterranean Sea. Nassau, Liverpool, Montpellier... Kat realised that she had always ended up living by the water!

After a few weeks, Kat's training regime began

to take shape. She woke early most days, with the sun streaming through the window – Montpellier, she discovered, was one of the sunniest cities in France. She ate a croissant and a fruit shake before cycling to the training ground. There, she warmed up in the gym before heading out to the track with Bertrand. They would focus on one or two events in the morning, working with Kat's training partners, Kevin and Antoinette.

After a hard morning's training, she would tone her body with a sauna and an ice bath. In the heat of Montpellier, Kat was coming to enjoy the freezing ice bath!

In the afternoon she would go to the park to read, sitting on her favourite bench and enjoying the warm sunshine. It felt almost like being on holiday!

Life was good and Kat could feel her confidence returning. With Jean-Yves and Bertrand's expert coaching, she was getting stronger in every event. And it would soon be time to put herself to the test again...

In February 2017, Kat travelled back to Sheffield for the British Athletics Indoor Team Trials. She was back on form. She jumped 6.69 metres in the long jump and, best of all, the smile was back on her face.

Watching from the sidelines, Bertrand was smiling too. It was great to see Kat enjoying herself. He knew that if she continued having fun, her scores would go up and up and up. There was no limit to what she could achieve.

'Well done,' he told her. 'I think you're all set for the World Championships in London.'

A flicker of anxiety passed across Kat's face as her mind recalled the disastrous competition in Beijing two years earlier.

Bertrand read her mind. 'That was then, this is now. Everything has changed.'

One thing hadn't changed though. Jess had retired from international competition, and fans and commentators were still be making the comparison between them:

'The new Jessica Ennis-Hill.'

'The heir.'

'Jess's successor.'

Could Kat live up to Jess's huge legacy? She felt an enormous weight of expectation on her shoulders.

'You are no longer in Jess's shadow, Kat,' Bertrand told her. 'Your scores are already better than Jess's. Now, you need to prove that you can perform in the spotlight.'

***

While Kat had always thought of wise, supportive Jess as a mentor and not a rival, now she had a true rival: Nafissatou Thiam, the Olympic champion. Nafi was two years younger than Kat. Where Kat was weakest, the Belgian athlete was strongest. Her throws were enormous: she excelled at both shot put and javelin. Kat was stronger in the sprint and 800 metres, but Nafi was rapidly catching up with her scores in the high jump and long jump.

Kat knew she would need all her strength and skill to beat this formidable opponent. Nafi was focused, she was consistent, and she seemed to be unshakeable under pressure. And Nafi would be hungry to win the World Championship in London to add to her Olympic victory.

The battle was on.

CHAPTER 19

LOSS AND RIVALRY

Run faster, sprint harder, fly higher, do yourself justice...

Kat's favourite mantra ran through her head as she walked out into the London Olympic stadium for the 2017 World Championships. This place had such happy memories! Her mind flew back to the 2012 Olympics. She had been just a teenager then. No pressure, only the joy of competing for a passionate home crowd. How different it was now.

But Kat felt ready. She felt strong after months of training in Montpellier. She knew she must shut the pressure out of her mind, and focus on her performance.

Kat didn't expect to win the hurdles. There were stronger hurdlers in the field. She just needed a good score – and blazing over the hurdles behind the faster runners, she got it. She finished sixth overall, almost equalling her personal best. *So far, so good!*

The high jump was next. As usual, Kat expected to pick up extra points in her strongest discipline. The height was set at 1.86 metres. Fixing her eyes on the bar, she was away, bounding along the run-up, springing higher with each step. But her jump was too short. The bar toppled.

No matter, thought Kat. She would get over it on her second attempt. Away she ran – but once again, her leap sent the crossbar falling to the ground.

Everything was riding on her final jump. *Fly higher, do yourself justice.*

She ran. She leapt. She felt the impact as her back hit the bar. Not again! The bar fell away as she tumbled to the landing mat. No! Another failed jump!

Kat remained on her knees on the mat, her head in her hands. She had run out of chances. When she finally got to her feet, the crowd gave her a warm cheer of support. But without a strong score in the high jump, Kat knew how hard it would be to claw her way to a medal. Not against competitors like these. Not against Nafi Thiam.

In the evening, under the floodlights, Kat won the 200 metres with ease. But back at her hotel that night, it was the high jump she was thinking of. She wept tears of shame and disappointment. She felt like she had let her fans down. Worst of all, she felt like she had let her mum down. She wanted so badly to make Tracey proud!

Day two dawned clear and sunny. Kat shone in the long jump, but lost points in the javelin. Once again, she would be going into the 800 metres race with little hope of a medal. The home crowd cheered her as she crossed the line second – but she knew her points were not enough.

Nafi Thiam finished the race last... but with

6,784 points, she still won the gold medal easily.

Kat finished fifth overall, with 6,558 points. Another world championships. Another disappointment.

I'm still not tough enough mentally, she thought to herself. *I'm still letting myself get thrown off course by one bad event. How can I learn to stay strong when things go wrong?*

* * *

Coming back from a bad jump was one thing. But in November, Kat got a call that would change everything.

Seven thousand miles away from Montpellier, in Nassau, her father, Ricky, had died.

The shock left Kat reeling. He was just 59. As she travelled to the Bahamas with Tracey to say a final goodbye, sadness and regret filled her mind.

She knew how proud her dad was of her. He had loved to see her compete.

Grieving for her kind, loving father, with his big

laugh and even bigger smile, was the hardest thing Kat had ever had to do.

***

Losing Ricky was a wake-up call for Kat. As she travelled back to France to resume her training, there was just one thing on her mind. Her dad would never see her compete again, but she would succeed for her mum. She would prove her critics wrong. She would push herself to victory, whatever it took. She was determined that her mum would see her win.

She could do it.

She *would* do it.

Out on the track, Bertrand could see the new determination on Kat's face. Inside her, a new self-confidence was building. Whenever she felt doubt creeping in, she thought of Ricky. She was learning resilience. From now on, she wouldn't let anything hold her back.

She was ready to bring her A-game.

*＊＊

Kat's next competition was the World Indoor Championships in Birmingham in March 2018. She always enjoyed the indoor events. After all, there was no javelin, and that suited her just fine!

Do yourself justice. Kat was determined that she would. After a hard-fought competition, Kat won gold, a much-needed confidence boost.

Next, Kat's sights were set on the Commonwealth Games on Australia's Gold Coast. Once again, she rocketed to victory. Another gold!

But Kat returned to Montpellier in pain. She had injured her calf at the competition. It was a huge blow – a whole month away from training!

In the past, this kind of setback would have left Kat struggling with self-doubt. But the new Kat was determined not to be downhearted. This time, she only looked forward.

Do yourself justice.

Next came the European Championships in Berlin. Kat had missed lots of training because of her injury, but – *Bring it on*, she thought. *Bring on Berlin*. Nafi would be there and she was eager to test herself against the formidable Belgian. She was ready to push herself to her limit.

Kat finished in second place, behind Nafi who took the gold medal. But Kat was happy. She had not let her injury bring her down. She had stayed strong. She had kept motivated. Every fibre of her body ached, but it felt amazing to be standing on the podium, receiving her silver medal, knowing that she had given it her all.

And there was more. Despite her injury, Kat had earned a personal best score of 6,759. She was now in the world all-time Top 25 heptathletes, alongside Nafi, Jess, Denise, and the highest-scoring heptathlete in history, the American Jackie Joyner-Kersee!

Kat had proved her abilities. She had earned her

place in the heptathlon hall of fame.

There was just one question remaining. Would she – *could* she – beat Nafi Thiam?

Bertrand certainly thought so. And so did one other important member of Team KJT: Daley Thompson. Daley was a former Olympic gold medallist and decathlon world champion. Kat valued his encouragement and straight-talking advice. How lucky she was to have so many amazing athletes who supported and believed in her: Daley, Denise, Jess...

'She's so strong. So consistent,' said Kat. 'She seems unbeatable.'

'No one is unbeatable,' said Daley. 'Anyone is beatable. Even me,' he joked.

Anyone is beatable. That sounded like a great new mantra. Kat turned it over in her head. *Anyone is beatable*.

'You need to see rivalry as positive, Kat. That's how you push you yourself. That's how you grow.'

If anyone knew the benefits of rivalry it was

Daley. His long rivalry with Jürgen Hingsen, the German decathlete, was legendary.

'You're second in the world now,' Daley continued. 'Use that. When you're number two, you try harder. You're hungrier to win.'

'Thanks, Daley.' Kat smiled. His advice had given her a way forward. Embrace rivalry!

'Doha is coming up. You are good enough to be world champion. Make it happen, Kat.'

The World Championships in Doha, Qatar, were just a few months away. Everything Kat did was build-up for that competition. Every step. Every jump. Every throw.

Kat nodded. Could this be her year? She had failed on the world championship stage so many times now. After all her disappointments, she wanted a medal so badly!

Anyone is beatable.

Kat smiled. She knew Nafi's weaknesses.

And more importantly, she knew her own strengths.

CHAPTER 20

DOHA DREAMS

Kat sat in the call room inside Doha's Khalifa International Stadium, Qatar. Along with 30 other heptathletes, she was waiting to be called to the track for the start of the 2019 World Championships.

She was surrounded by familiar faces. Most of these women had been competing against her for years now. It was almost like a family, thought Kat. Unlike the sprinters, who often tried to intimidate each other before races, to psyche each other out, the heptathletes always had friendly words for one another. They respected each other. The heptathlon was simply too gruelling for mind games!

Kat glanced at Nafi. While groups of other athletes chatted, the Belgian athlete was sitting on her own, as she usually did before events. Nafi was always friendly, always polite, but she liked to remain inside her own quiet bubble before competing.

It certainly seems to work, thought Kat.

Because of the sweltering daytime temperatures in Qatar – up to 40 degrees even in September – most events were being held in the evenings and late into the night. Many athletes and coaches grumbled. But not Kat. She was a night owl. She found early-morning starts much harder!

When the athletes were finally called into the stadium, Kat had a broad smile on her face. The pressure was definitely on. Along with Dina Asher-Smith in the 100 metres and Laura Muir in the 1,500 metres, Kat was one of the favourites for a British medal. But she was learning to take pressure in her stride. After so many years feeling dread every time she stepped into an arena, now she felt bubbling excitement once again, just like she had as a teenager.

* * *

Up in the stands, Kat's most loyal and passionate supporter was ready and waiting. Tracey had watched all of Kat's competitions over the years. She had sat in hundreds of arenas and had seen Kat's confidence grow and crash again and again over the years. It filled her with joy to see her daughter happy and enjoying sport again. She prayed that Kat's hard work and determination would pay off this time.

Suddenly a ripple of applause started up. There they were! Tracey's heart gave a lurch as she spotted her daughter down on the track. The feeling of pride at seeing Kat in an international championship had never lessened. And the feeling of anxiety didn't either! Already her fingers were gripping the seat in front of her. *Relax!* she told herself. *They're not even on the blocks yet!*

Down by the start line, Kat was limbering up for the hurdles. Her scores were getting stronger in this race, whereas it was one of Nafi's weaker events. A win should be hers. Should be. Kat knew to take nothing for granted.

She planted her feet in the blocks and steadied her nerves. *Go!*

Kat was off, eating up the ground with every pace, striding gracefully over the hurdles. She overtook the leader, Annie Kunz, as they reached halfway, then she sprinted to the finish, well clear of the rest of the runners. Her time: 13.09 seconds. A personal best!

Kat's hands flew to her face and she let out a laugh of surprise and delight. Up in the stands, Tracey gave a whoop of joy. It was the perfect start!

But how would Kat fare in the high jump? It was here that her medal chances had unexpectedly crumbled at the World Championships in London two years ago.

Kat cleared the lower heights easily. The bar was

now set at 1.95 metres. She bounded along the run-up then leapt. For an instant, she seemed to hover in the air above the pole, before curling gracefully over the top and falling back on to the mat below. *Phew! Clear!*

Nafi Thiam cleared the same height, gaining the same points. But Kat was still in the lead thanks to her spectacular hurdles performance.

In the shot put, Nafi performed brilliantly as usual. An epic throw of 15.22 metres put her first in the event, and first on the overall leader board, overtaking Kat.

Kat knew she couldn't match Nafi's throw, but she needed to score well.

Her first and second throws were unimpressive: 12.33 and 12.38 metres respectively. She had just one attempt left. Kat visualised the throw, then used her force to hurl the shot strongly away. It landed with a thud at 13.86 metres: another personal best! Kat could barely believe it. She stared at the replay on the stadium screen. It was true! The throw of her lifetime! She spun around to beam at Bertrand, bouncing up and down with delight.

A personal best in the shot put? Who knew!

Nafi was still in the lead, thanks to her huge throw. But Kat was now only 51 points behind. Winning her 200-metres heat easily, Kat was soon back on top, leading Nafi by 96 points.

Day one was over.

It was late into the night as the athletes finally left the arena to return to their hotels. The beautiful curved stadium was lit up in glowing rainbow colours, while the sports complex around it dazzled with lights, like a fairy grotto. Beyond the city on one side was the Persian Gulf, on the other, the desert.

Kat was tired. She was hungry. But above all she was excited.

I *can win this*, she thought. *I can actually win this!*

CHAPTER 21

GOLD
GLORY

When Kat woke the next morning, there were still hours to wait before the start of the competition. All the action would begin at dusk when the searing desert heat had lessened. There was something magical about performing at night, like being in a dream, Kat thought.

When day two's events finally began, it was with the long jump. It was her moment to put the pain of Beijing behind her. It was her moment to shine.

Kat flew down the runway, arms pumping. Springing from the take-off board, she hurled herself over the sand. She could barely bring herself to look up and check the colour of the flag. *Please don't be red!*

But the white flag was waving. The jump was clean – and long: 6.77 metres.

Phew! Kat now led Nafi by 216 points.

But the javelin was next. Nafi would score big, she knew.

Kat was first to throw, and she gave herself another cause to smile. Yet another personal best: 43.93 metres! On the sidelines, Bertrand flung his fist in the air in celebration. Nafi, who had an injury to her elbow, still beat her, but her throw was well short of a personal best. Kat would be difficult to beat now.

Sitting in the stands, Tracey dared to imagine a gold medal around Kat's neck.

Down on the track, as she prepared for the 800 metres, Kat did too. *Run faster. Sprint harder. Do yourself justice.*

But before they could run the final race of the

World Championships, there was the stadium light show. Since all the events in Doha were taking place at night, the organisers made full use of the dramatic night-time setting. Before each event, the arena plunged into darkness. Music played and coloured lights danced across the stadium while the competitors were introduced. As Kat was announced by loudspeaker, her name was projected onto the track in huge capital letters, while glowing ribbons of red, white and blue light rippled around the arena.

Finally the booming soundtrack ended and the floodlights came to life again, returning the arena to brightness. It was time.

The starting gun fired. Verena Preiner from Austria set a fast pace out of the blocks. Kat joined her at the front, along with the two American runners, Kendell Williams and Erica Bougard. The group of four pulled steadily away from the rest, with Kat running in third, behind Verena and Kendell. She was calculating her strategy with every stride. She needed to get ahead of them, but not too soon. It was always easier to have someone else to set the pace. But if she left it too long to overtake, Verena or Kendell might pull away – or Erica might steal her position in third. She would have to make her move soon...

Okay, now!

Kat summoned an extra burst of energy. Quick as a flash, she darted into the narrow space between the two leading runners, overtaking first Kendell, then Verena. As the bell rang to signal halfway, she was already pulling away from them. Would they fall back? Would they keep up with her? Would one of them find a final spurt of energy and challenge her for the lead? All she knew was that she had to keep the pace up. Being out in front made her vulnerable, blind to the action behind her. She couldn't – *wouldn't* – let anyone overtake!

With 250 metres to go, Kat accelerated again. Her long legs carried her flying down the home strait. She sensed she was increasing her lead over the others. She urged her tired legs onwards, faster, faster.

Come on! Come on! Over the line!

Kat jogged to a halt, stopped to catch her breath, then flung herself onto the track. She had done it! She lay there panting for several moments. Behind her, the other runners were tumbling across the line and falling to their knees, sprawling across the lanes. With seven gruelling events completed, every single one of them was exhausted!

Gold!

Kat had given it her all. She had won and – wait! Another personal best: 2 minutes 7.26 seconds! What a way to end the competition!

It had been an extraordinary two nights. A gold medal. Four personal bests. A victory over Nafi Thiam at last!

And with 6,981 points in total, she had also overtaken Jessica Ennis-Hill as the highest-scoring British heptathlete of all time.

When tears came to Kat's eyes, they were of joy.

Up in the stands, Tracey also had tears in her eyes. Her humble, hard-working daughter was world champion. *World champion!* Tracey had believed in Kat every step of the way, from the moment she exchanged ballet shoes for running shoes. She could not have been prouder of her amazing daughter!

On the sidelines, jubilant texts and tweets were piling into Kat's phone. From Jodie, Daley, Denise, Jess, Barrie Wells... everyone who had been on this incredible journey with her wanted to share this special moment. Kat was itching to read their messages of love and support.

But before she could do that, there was the small matter of the medal ceremony.

Kat had collected many medals over the years. She had stood on many podiums. But her first world championship medal was truly special. The proudest moment of her life so far.

And Doha did things a little differently with its ceremony.

Instead of a podium on the field, with the crowd

looking down on the athletes, Kat and her fellow medalists stood on a huge illuminated plinth, at the very top of the arena. Behind them were giant screens, each with an animated national flag, and huge CGI medals – a gold disc for Kat, a silver for Nafi and a bronze for Verena Preiner. There were real medals too, of course. Kat beamed with delight as her gold medal was placed around her neck. As the National Anthem began to play, more happy tears flowed down her cheeks. It was the moment she had been dreaming of – world championship glory at last.

This is for you, Mum, thought Kat.

CHAPTER 22

BRINGING IT HOME

Doha had put on a dazzling light show, but Liverpool was not to be outdone. To celebrate Kat's victory, the monuments of her hometown were lit up in red, white and blue. A giant gold medal hung from the town hall balcony, along with a huge banner: *Congratulations Katarina Johnson-Thompson*. Kat was the first person from the city ever to win a world championship medal – it was time to celebrate!

And, following her victory in Doha, it was becoming impossible for Kat to walk around Liverpool without being recognised.

'Katarina!'

'KJT!'

'Congratulations, Kat!'

'Our girl!'

Kat had never signed so many autographs or posed for so many selfies.

And the people of Liverpool weren't the only ones eager to welcome their homecoming champion.

'Bronx! Chorizo! Have you missed me?' called Kat as she stepped over the threshold of her mum's house, now home to her two beloved dachshunds.

The sound of eight small paws scampering wildly through the house told her that they had! The two dogs tumbled excitedly into her arms, nuzzling her, licking her, barking with delight. Kat adored sun-drenched Montpellier, but it would never have what Liverpool did: snuggles with her favourite furry duo.

'It's so good to see you, boys!'

Of course, Bronx and Chorizo had no idea of her achievements halfway across the world in Doha. And it seemed, they were the only inhabitants of

Liverpool who weren't interested in her medal.

'Look, Bronx! Look what Mummy won!' Kat took the precious gold medal from its box and dangled it in front of him. Bronx gave a suspicious sniff then pattered away.

'How about you, Chorizo? Don't you want to know what Mummy gets up to when she's not here cuddling you?'

No, Chorizo didn't. The shiny thing wasn't edible, and it wasn't a tennis ball.

Kat grinned at Tracey. 'They don't want me to get big-headed, do they!'

Tracey laughed. 'Your nan will want to show it to the neighbours, as usual.'

Kat giggled. Her nan had always showed off her medals, ever since her very first youth championships. Her family was so proud and it meant the world to her.

Kat fondled her dogs. 'Deep down I know you care too, boys,' she joked.

* * *

And there was more exciting news to come. In November, Kat was shortlisted for the BBC Sports Personality of the Year. The show would be broadcast live from Aberdeen on 15th December. The news was announced on social media by the Liverpool FC players Trent Alexander-Arnold and Alex Oxlade-Chamberlain.

'Sports personality of the year?' gasped Kat. 'But—' She could hardly believe it. She had watched the show since she was a child. Past nominees and winners included so many of her sporting heroes. 'Am I a sporting hero? Really?'

It didn't seem possible!

Kat's fellow nominees were Ben Stokes, Dina Asher-Smith, Raheem Sterling, Lewis Hamilton and Alun Wyn Jones. What an honour it was to be named alongside these incredible sportspeople.

On the morning of the show, Kat travelled back from Martinique where she had been training.

Her first stop was Aberdeen Children's Hospital. The children, who had spent months in the hospital, had written to Kat, asking if she would visit them.

Yes, of course she would! And she wanted it to be a surprise.

'Girls, boys, we have a visitor,' announced the chief nurse. 'Can you guess who it is?'

Walking into the surgical ward, Kat's heart leapt as she saw the stunned faces of her young fans. There were squeals and whoops and cheers. *Katarina! Katarina! KJT!*

'That was an amazing welcome, thank you, everyone!' smiled Kat.

The children had been joined by their parents and carers. Kat talked to everyone, signed autographs and posed for more selfies. Then she spotted a table football set. 'Who likes football?' she asked.

A little boy, Morgan, piped up. 'Me, I do!'

'Me too,' said Kat. 'I challenge you to a game, Morgan. Do you want to be red or blue?'

Morgan picked red. 'Because Aberdeen play in red.'

Kat grinned. 'So do Liverpool. But I guess I'll have to be blue this time.'

They took up their positions. The other children watched as they swung their plastic players back and forth, sending the ball from one end of the tiny pitch to the other.

'Goal!' whooped Morgan as he shot the ball past Kat's goalie.

'Goal!' shouted Kat as she scored a few seconds later.

But Morgan had the upper hand. The children giggled at Kat's dismay as she let in goal after goal. 'This is harder than it looks,' she laughed. 'Morgan, you're a worthy winner!'

'I beat KJT!' he whooped. 'I actually beat KJT!'

It was time to say goodbye. Kat was due at the BBC studio. Filming would start in just a few hours.

'Good luck, Kat!' shouted the children, their families and their nurses. 'We hope you win.'

'Meeting you lot, I've won already!' Kat grinned.

***

Kat was bubbling with excitement that night. The Sports Personality of the Year was so much more than a competition. She loved hearing the inspiring stories of sportspeople and coaches, who were making a difference in so many amazing ways.

This year's award for Unsung Hero went to Keiren Thompson from Nottingham, who ran a project called Helping Kids Achieve. His work gave confidence and motivation to so many young people.

The lifetime achievement award went to Tanni Grey-Thompson, who had championed paralympic sport for 30 years.

It was incredible to be on a stage with these inspiring people!

Finally, it was time to announce the main award, Sports Personality of the Year. The iconic trophy was ridden into the studio on a quadricycle by former rugby player Gareth Thomas, along with cricketer Graham Swann, and former athlete Dame Kelly Holmes, another hero of Kat's.

Ben should win this, she thought. *I think Ben will win.*

She was right. The trophy was won by Ben Stokes. The cricketer had had an outstanding year, leading his team to victory after victory. Kat cheered louder than anyone as he collected the trophy. The second worthy winner of the day!

And Kat knew she was also a winner. Being here in Aberdeen for this wonderful celebration, well, it was the perfect end to a perfect year!

* * *

But what about the future?

Kat would be part of the British squad travelling to Tokyo for the Games. Her greatest rival remained the Olympic champion, Nafi Thiam. To beat Nafi at the Olympics, Kat knew she would have to do something that no other British heptathlete had ever done: score over 7,000 points. She would have to excel not just in the jumps, but in everything. Even the shot put!

Could Kat do it? Well, she had learned how to deal with pressure and overcome setbacks. She was faster and stronger than ever. Her coach believed in her. Her friends and family believed in her. Most importantly, she believed in herself. A medal, even a gold, was now within her grasp.

Bring it on, thought Kat. *Bring on Tokyo. I'm ready!*

World Championship Medals

🏆 Sopot 2014: Long jump, Silver

🏆 Birmingham 2018: Pentathlon, Gold

🏆 Doha 2019: Heptathlon, Gold

NAME:	Katarina Johnson-Thompson
DATE OF BIRTH:	**9 January 1993**
PLACE OF BIRTH:	Liverpool, UK
NATIONALITY:	**British**
SPORT:	Athletics
Height:	**183 cm**
Main events:	Heptathlon
Club:	**Liverpool Harriers**
Coach:	Bertrand Valcin

Olympic Medals

GOLD SILVER  BRONZE

World Championship Medals

GOLD SILVER BRONZE

Turn the page for a sneak preview

of another brilliant story in

the Ultimate Sports Heroes series...

TOM DALEY

Available now!

CHAPTER 1

BUDAPEST BRILLIANCE

22 July 2017

Tom Daley could barely breathe as he watched his rival, Chen Aisen, poised on the edge of the platform. It was the final of the men's 10-metre platform event at the World Aquatic Championships in Budapest and the tension around the pool was electric. Tom led Chen by a margin of just 5.7 points, but both divers had one more dive to perform. With so little difference between their scores, anything could happen. Tom swallowed nervously. He could see the determination and focus in his rival's eyes. If the Chinese diver – the Olympic champion – delivered a spectacular dive, the gold medal could easily slip from Tom's grasp.

The crowd hushed. Chen leapt from the board and into the air, turning a series of elegant somersaults before dropping neatly into the pool. Cheers rang around the auditorium. Tom gulped. It was a spectacular dive. His eyes flicked to the scoreboard: 106.20. A huge score! It would be very hard to beat.

Chen clambered from the pool, grinning. His teammates clustered around him, buzzing with noisy congratulations. Chen didn't even glance at Tom, standing on the top platform. *He thinks he's won,* Tom realised. *They don't think I can beat him. Well. We'll see about that.*

Tom's competitive spark had been lit. Adrenaline surged through him. He knew he would need the dive of his life to beat Chen. But he had nothing to lose. He would give his all in this final dive.

Here goes.

For a fraction of a second, it felt to Tom as though he was flying, soaring above the pool with his arms stretched out like wings. As gravity started to tug him downwards, he gripped his knees to his chest and tipped into his first somersault. Round and round he spun, suspended in mid-air, faster, faster. As he tumbled out of his final somersault, the only direction was down, down, down, plummeting at top speed towards the shimmering blue pool below.

As Tom hit the water, an explosion of cheers rocked the auditorium. Up in the stands, Tom's mum, Debbie, let out a cry of delight. Tom's husband, Lance, flung his arms into the air, while at the side of the pool, Tom's coach, Jane, jumped up and down for joy and his Great Britain teammates shrieked and whooped.

Tom could hear the cacophony of sound as he kicked back to the surface.

Was it good? It must have been good for the crowd to be cheering like this!

With eyes on the scoreboard, he blinked in disbelief: 106.20 points. The same score as Chen! It was enough to keep him on top. He had done it. He had beaten the Olympic champion.

Tom ran straight to Jane and gave her a joyful hug. She had supported and believed in him every step of the way. His teammates crowded round, bombarding him with hugs and kisses.

Meanwhile, his amazing mum and his wonderful husband, his most loyal supporters, were hurrying down from the stands, waiting to fling their arms around the new world champion. Tom felt like he was being swept up in a tidal wave of love, pride and support. He couldn't take the smile off his face. The victory was his. But it also belonged to his family, his friends, his teammates, his coach, his physiotherapist, his fans... everyone who had come on this incredible journey with him.

And at just 23, Tom knew he had much, much more to give. This journey wasn't over yet!